Cycle Repair
Step by Step

by Rob van der Plas

SPRINGFIELD BOOKS LIMITED

Published by Springfield Books Limited, Norman Road, Denby Dale, Huddersfield HD8 8TH, West Yorkshire, Great Britain

Original text copyright © 1986/87 Falken-Verlag GmbH, 6272 Niedernhausen/Taunus, West Germany

English translation copyright © 1988 Springfield Books Limited, Norman Road, Denby Dale, Huddersfield HD8 8TH, West Yorkshire, Great Britain

First edition 1988

British Library Cataloguing in Publication Data

Plas, Rob van der
Cycle repair step by step.
1. Bicycles. Maintenance & repair –
Amateurs' manuals
I. Title II. Fahrrad Reparaturen
English
629.28' 772

ISBN: 0 947655 44 1

Acknowledgements

Photos: Photo-Design-Studio Gerhard Burock

Cover photograph: Julie's Cycle Shop, Leicester/Ian Wood Photography

Diagrams: Rob van der Plas

Design: Main-Taunus-Satz, Giebitz & Kleber GmbH, Eschborn/Taunus, West Germany

Cover design: Douglas Martin Associates

Translation: Andrew Shackleton/Asgard Publishing Services

Technical adviser on English edition: Steve Snowling

The author and publishers also wish to thank Dieter Worth of Frankfurt and Fritz Reitz of Wiesbaden for providing the bicycles that are featured in the photos.

The information in this book has been carefully checked by, and on behalf of, the author and publishers, but they can accept no liability for damages to persons or to property.

Printed in Germany by Offset-Druck Zumbrink, Bad Salzuflen

Contents

4

Introduction to cycle maintenance

The purpose of this book is to help you to keep your bicycle in tiptop condition. It is not about bikes generally, so don't expect to read about the history of the bicycle, or about subjects such as fitness or touring. But this general introduction may be helpful in providing the background you will need in order to know how to use the various tools. The more familiar you are with your machine, the more easily you will understand the instructions later in the book.

The different parts of the bicycle

Figure **1*** below shows the names of the different parts of the bicycle. All of them will crop up repeatedly in later chapters.

Here is a general description of the main component groups and fittings to be found on all types of bicycle. The classification is similar to that used in later chapters on repair and maintenance.

* **1** = Figure 1, etc.

The frame

·The frame is the main structure or 'skeleton' of the bicycle on which all the other parts are then mounted (see page 21 **3**). The frame consists of two main sections: a front section made up of four fairly thick tubes − the *down tube*, the *top tube*, the *seat tube* and the *head tube*; and a back section consisting of two pairs of narrower tubes − the *chainstays* and *seat stays*. The short horizontal tube at the bottom is called the *bottom bracket shell*.

The steering

The steering system is made up of the front forks and handlebars, together with the headset, where the steering column turns in the frame. The bars can be raised or lowered using an adjustable clamp mechanism. In many models the bar angle can also be adjusted.

The saddle

The saddle is mounted on the seat pillar, which in turn is inserted into the seat tube. Again there are various clamp mechanisms for adjusting the height, position and angle of the saddle.

The transmission

The transmission of a bike is the system which transmits power from the rider's feet to the back wheel. It is made up of several elements. The first is the *bottom bracket*, which is attached to the bottom bracket shell. An axle runs through it to which the *cranks* are fixed. The *pedals* are then screwed onto the cranks. The right crank is attached to the *chainwheel* (or several chainwheels in the case of derailleur gears). The *chain* runs from the chainwheel to the rear-wheel sprocket. Finally, there is the freewheel mechanism, which is really part of the gear system.

The gears

Most modern bikes are equipped with a gear system. This controls the ratio between the pedal speed and the travelling speed and between the pedal power and the travelling power.

Most bikes for general use have *hub gears*. These are integrated into the rear-wheel hub, and are often combined

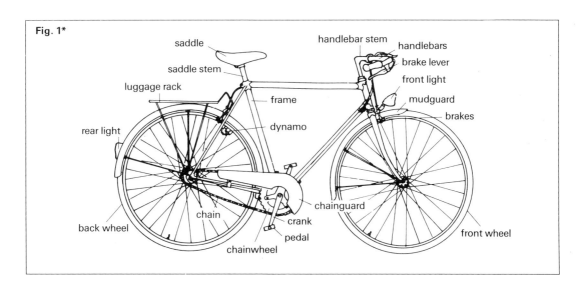

Fig. 1*

saddle · handlebar stem · handlebars · brake lever · front light · mudguard · brakes · saddle stem · luggage rack · frame · dynamo · rear light · chainguard · back wheel · chain · crank · pedal · chainwheel · front wheel

with a back-pedal brake. Hub gears are controlled by a lever attached to the handlebars. This is linked to the hub via a flexible cable that runs through guides attached to the frame.

Derailleur gears are used primarily on racing bikes. The usual mechanism involves two or three different-sized chainwheels attached to the bottom bracket, and a freewheel consisting of five, six or seven different-sized sprockets attached to the hub. The *derailleur* transfers the chain from one rear-wheel sprocket to another, while the *front changer* moves the chain between the different chainwheels. The gears are again controlled by means of levers and cables, although the levers are usually attached to the down tube instead of the handlebars.

The wheels

The *hub* in the centre of each wheel turns on bearings around an axle that runs through either the front forks or the back part of the frame. The hub is linked by *spokes* to the *rim* of the wheel, on which the *tyre* rests. A conventional tyre consists of an airtight inner tube and a resilient outer covering. Racing bikes are equipped with tubular or 'sew-up' tyres, which are cemented onto special rims.

The brakes

All bikes must be fitted with two independent brakes.

The back wheel may often have a *hub brake*. This is usually a back-pedal brake,

but may be a drum brake or, very rarely, a disc brake. The pedal brake is engaged by pedalling backwards, while the other types are linked to hand levers. The hand levers normally work via a flexible cable, although occasionally stiff rods are used.

Rim brakes are always used on the front wheel, and often on the back wheel too, especially on racing bikes. They work excellently in good conditions, being strong, direct and finely tuned. But they are sensitive to water or dirt, and require much more maintenance than hub brakes. Rim brakes also come in several different forms (see page 67 [1]).

Lights

The lights are probably the most important additional fittings, and the most vulnerable too. In some countries a dynamo system is legally required, while in others battery-powered lights may be sufficient.

Battery lights normally consist of two independent units, each with its own battery. A dynamo system consists of a direct-current dynamo linked by insulated wires to both front and back lights. The current is fed back to the dynamo via the metal of the bicycle frame.

The other vital element of the lighting system is the back reflector.

Accessories

All the other fittings are optional apart from an audible warning device – usually a

bell, but sometimes a horn or klaxon. Some cyclists want all kinds of things; others prefer just the bare essentials.

Most bikes are equipped with mudguards, chainguard, luggage rack and prop stand. Extras might include a child seat, a clothes protector, a rear-view mirror, a small trailer, and baskets or bags attached to the handlebars, saddle or luggage rack.

But the most important things are always the easiest to forget: the tyre pump and the tools.

Workshop and tools

You won't need very many tools to carry out most of the necessary repairs, and a small workroom should be quite sufficient. Some jobs will inevitably need to be done elsewhere, maybe in the middle of a ride; but it is still very much easier if you have a dedicated workshop with all the special equipment on hand.

The workshop

Your bicycle workshop must be at least two metres square and well lit. You will also need a workbench with a vice, a set of wall shelves with special places for individual tools, and drawers for storing all the smaller items.

The bike itself can be either hung up on the wall or placed on the floor [2]. But you should be careful not to

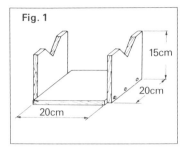

Fig. 1

15cm

20cm

20cm

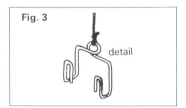

Fig. 3

detail

Fig. 2

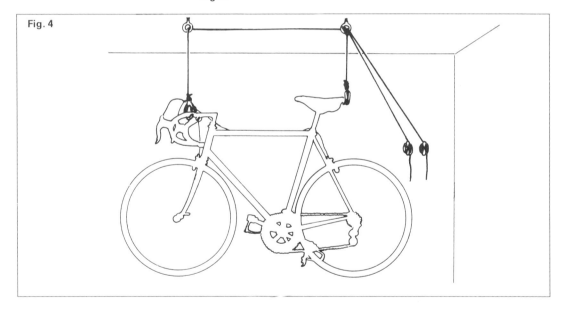

Fig. 4

damage the handlebar fittings, especially the brake cables, which can easily become trapped or broken. You can make your own handlebar rest **1** or a pulley system for hanging the bike on **3** **4**. Both of these will prevent you from damaging your machine.

The tools

Many jobs require special equipment, but most of them can be done with only a small basic set of tools. This section includes all the general tools that you can't possibly manage without.

The kinds of tools that you take when riding or touring will depend very much on individual circumstances. Think carefully about what might go wrong, and the kinds of tools or spares you might need.

When buying your tools, bear in mind that they vary greatly in quality and price. If you go for the more expensive options, they will usually pay for themselves in the long run.

There are two basic categories of tools: universal tools and specialist bicycle tools. The latter can only be bought at specialist bicycle shops. We shall limit ourselves here to the universal tools ☐; special tools ☐ are dealt with later in relation to the jobs they are needed for.

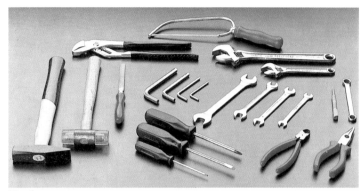

Fig. 1

Screwdrivers

A set of 4–7mm screwdrivers are sufficient for the normal slit-headed screws. One or two cross-head screwdrivers are also needed.

Spanners

These are used for turning hexagonal nuts and bolts or screw-in parts with flattened grip surfaces. You will need two adjustable spanners (about 15cm and 20–25cm long respectively), plus two sets of ordinary spanners (7–15mm), one set open-ended and the other ringed.

Fig. 2

Allen keys

These are needed for any special screw or bicycle part with a hexagonal recess in the head (sizes 4–8mm).

Hammers

You will need an ordinary hammer weighing about 300g, plus a light hammer with a plastic or wooden head.

Hacksaw

A small hacksaw is quite sufficient for small jobs such as

restoring a worn screw slit or separating damaged parts that have become rusted together.

Pliers

These should not be used for jobs that can be done better with other tools. Pliers are no substitute for a spanner, for example. Needle-nosed and offset pliers are very useful, and also a pipe wrench.

Files and wire brushes

You will occasionally need a small flat or round file to even out damaged or protruding parts. Files and wire brushes can also be used for cleaning screw joints and other parts that are rusted up.

Measuring tools ☐

A Vernier caliper is essential for accurately measuring all the parts that you buy or instal. When you buy one, ask the assistant to explain how it is used to measure lengths, widths, thicknesses, depths and recesses to within 0.1mm. A retractable metal measuring tape will also be needed.

Cleaning tools

All you need are a few cloths and small brushes (including paintbrushes), plus some steel wool or a pan scourer.

Lubrication fluids

You will need ballbearing grease, a mineral oil such as motor oil, a special chain lubricant, and a spray can of thin oil for greasing bare metal

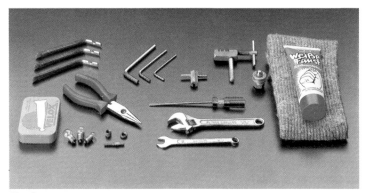

Fig. 3

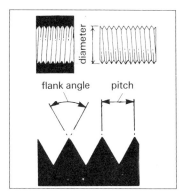

Fig. 6

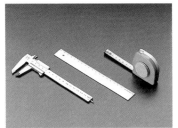

Fig. 4

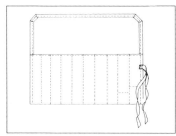

Fig. 5

Leave a few compartments free for any possible additions. The tyre pump and any larger spares will need to be stored in other places on your bicycle.

parts of the frame. Vaseline and metal wax are also needed for these areas.

Cleaning fluids

Apart from water and soap, you will also need a solvent such as white spirit, turpentine or paraffin. The solvent should be mixed with up to 5% of mineral oil so as to prevent rust after washing. Metal polish is needed for parts finished with chrome or aluminium.

Travelling tools

You must decide for yourself what tools to take riding with you. On day-trips I take only the bare essentials: tyre pump, tyre removers, mending gear etc; a small

screwdriver and adjustable spanner; a cloth, a tube of hand-cleaning cream and some spare lightbulbs **3**.

On a longer tour abroad you have to be prepared for everything. Take your time to think of all tools you might need and in what sizes, and all the spares you could possibly require. List them as you go, and then take all of these items with you.

Gather up all the tools you have chosen and sort them out in front of you. Then wrap them up in a cloth or a wallet made of stiff material. Figure **5** shows what such a wallet might look like. There must be enough space between the tools to allow the wallet to be rolled up.

The basics of maintenance

The first principle of bicycle maintenance is this: however complete the instructions are, don't just follow them blindly. You should always think for yourself a bit. Even the best instructions can't hope to cover every detail or exception for every single kind of bike. So examine every instruction carefully to see how it should be adapted to suit your own particular case.

Screw fittings

Many parts of the bike, including individual components and fittings, involve some kind of screw mechanism. A screw fitting **6** consists of a round shank with a thread around the outside and a recess with a thread around the inside.

Each thread consists of a spiral groove with a triangular cross-section. The inner and outer threads should be closely matched so that the parts can be easily screwed in or out (provided the fittings are neither dirty, rusty nor damaged).

When the parts are fully screwed in, the two threads lock tightly together, creating a really strong bond (held together by friction). Inserting a washer below a nut, or a screw or bolt head, helps to lessen the friction and makes it easier to tighten the screw.

Many of the screw fittings on a bike are specially threaded. But they can be described according to the following features:

Nominal diameter

The diameter of the outer thread is expressed in millimetres or inches (the corresponding inner thread is slightly smaller.

Pitch

The pitch of a screw is the average distance between two neighbouring grooves of the thread. It is expressed either in millimetres or in threads per inch (TPI).

Flank angle

There are two standards for this: the usual 60° angle, and the Whitworth Fine Norm or BSF (British Standard Fine)

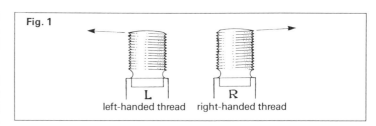

Fig. 1

L
left-handed thread

R
right-handed thread

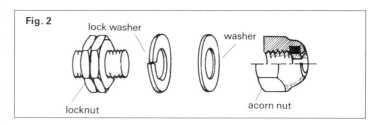

Fig. 2

lock washer

washer

locknut

acorn nut

with 55°, which is marked with an F.

Direction of thread 1

A right-handed thread (clockwise to tighten, anticlockwise to loosen) is more usual but not universal. Some parts of a bike such as the left pedal require a left-handed thread (anticlockwise to tighten, clockwise to loosen).

Not many manufacturers give this information clearly on their products, so you will often find that parts don't match. The best way to avoid this is to take the old part and the part which fits it to the bicycle shop with you. You can then try out the new part to make sure it fits.

For more detailed information about the kinds of thread used in bicycle parts, turn to the table on page 109.

All threads should be completely clean, undamaged and free from corrosion. First remove any dirt or rust with a fine wire brush, and then grease the thread with some acid-free vaseline, oil or grease.

When screwing parts in or out, hold one part firm and turn the other. Never use pliers, and make sure you use a tool that fits.

A correctly held spanner provides more leverage (and hence effective force) than a screwdriver or a wrongly held spanner. Hold the spanner as nearly as possible at right angles to the screw shank. When you are screwing a part directly into the frame, use the leverage provided by the frame. When screwing other parts, try to turn the part held by the spanner with the longest handle, and hold on with the screwdriver or the shorter tool. This only applies at the final tightening stage, when the greatest force is required.

There are several means of preventing screws from inad-

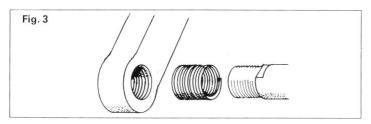

Fig. 3

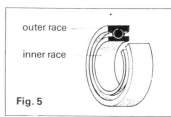

outer race

inner race

Fig. 5

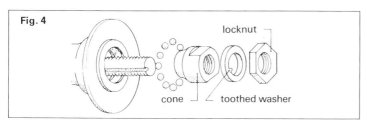

Fig. 4

locknut

cone   toothed washer

vertently coming loose, including lock washers, acorn nuts and locknuts ②. When a manufacturer has used them on a fitting, you should always replace them on reassembly. And you can always add them yourself when replacing a part that has unexpectedly come loose.

A *lock washer* is a specially shaped washer made of spring steel. It is pushed together under the pressure of the nut, making a bond that remains firm even if the nut comes loose owing to vibrations. Don't forget to put an ordinary washer under every nut, screw or bolt.

An *acorn nut* is also very effective. It has a firm plastic mounting that moulds to the end of the screw. It is specially recommended when fixing small items such as brake mountings.

A *locknut* is an extra nut that is screwed up against the main nut to create a really strong bond. It should

nonetheless be checked occasionally and tightened if necessary. Sometimes a part has to be allowed to turn slightly, in which case the main nut should only be moderately tightened but should then be held tightly by the locknut.

You should replace any screw fittings that keep coming loose or can't be properly tightened. First try to solve the problem by using a new nut or screw; if that doesn't work, replace both parts. In emergencies you can sometimes screw an extra nut over the top until both items can be replaced.

If the damaged thread is inside one of the larger parts of the bike, then you can temporarily replace the screw with a longer one that can be held in with an extra nut. Later you can rebore the hole and use a spiral thread insert or *Helicoil* ③.

Bearings

Practically all the moving parts of a bike are fitted with bearings, all of which need very careful maintenance. Specific instructions are given in later chapters, but there are some general principles to be observed.

There are two types of bearings used in bicycles. The removable type ④ is the commonest, but nowadays the bottom bracket, pedals and hubs are sometimes fitted with sealed bearings ⑤.

If one of the moving parts becomes loose or difficult to turn, or starts making horrid noises, this means the bearings are faulty. Removable bearings can be repaired. Sealed bearings will need to be completely replaced (though they are damaged less often, being better protected against water and dirt); this is an expert job requiring special tools, and you should leave it to a specialised mechanic.

Figure ④ shows how removable bearings are made up, and gives the names of the different components. The space in which the balls are housed is filled with ball bearing grease. The balls should not be too tightly packed. If

Fig. 1

Fig. 2

Fig. 3

this is the case, then one should be removed.

If the balls are held in a ball race or cage **1**, then this should be inserted so that only the balls (and not the metal cage) are touching the cup and cone. I personally recommend replacing the ball cage with loose balls of the corresponding size (see the table on page 108).

If the bearings are too loose, then the adjustable part needs tightening (usually the cone but sometimes the cup). To do this you first remove the locknut and then the locking ring that prevents the cone (or cup) from moving. The cone (or cup) can then be tightened or loosened. Finally the locking ring and locknut should be replaced **2**, but without moving the cone (or cup) in the process.

When bearings are overhauled, all the individual components should be removed, cleaned and greased. Any parts which are damaged or corroded should be replaced by new ones. It is always advisable to swap old balls for new ones, as wear is usually invisible to the naked eye.

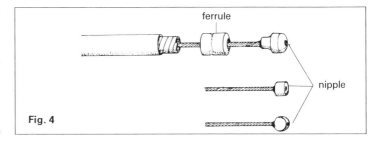

ferrule

nipple

Fig. 4

When reassembling the parts, you should fill the space between the cup and cone with grease before pushing the balls back in. The bearings should be adjusted so that they turn freely without any play.

Brake and gear cables

Bowden cables are used in both the brake and the gear systems. These are flexible cables made of plaited steel wire which take up the traction power of the brake or gear levers. The wires are usually passed through a flexible outer cable made of spiralled steel covered in plastic. But they can instead be passed (for the whole or part of their length) through special guides mounted along the frame.

The lever end of each cable has a nipple attached **4**. The opposite end is anchored to the brake **6** or changer **5**, and is cut off 2–3cm beyond the anchor bolt using offset pliers or a specialised tool for the purpose **3**. The whole length of the inner cable should be wiped with a cloth soaked in vaseline before it is passed through the outer cable (or the guides along the frame).

The inner cable comes in a variety of strengths, and there are several different types of nipple. So whenever you replace a cable, make sure you use the same type as before. It is advisable to keep spare cable of every kind that you will need, plus a roll of outer cable. And when you go on a long tour, take at least some brake cable with you.

Fig. 5

Fig. 6

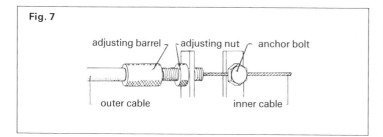

Fig. 7

adjusting barrel — adjusting nut — anchor bolt

outer cable — inner cable

same procedure as before. If there is no adjusting barrel (as with many derailleur gear changers, for example), you simply shorten the length of cable held by the anchor bolt.

Soldering

Soldering the ends of inner cables or electrical wires will help prevent them fraying. Cable ends should be soldered along the last 2—4cm of the end which is to be anchored. Electrical wires should only be soldered if they are to be held in grip contacts. If they are to be held in screw contacts, then a ring should be attached around the strands.

Equipment

- an electric soldering iron with a power of at least 60W
- some solder
- some emery paper.

Procedure

1. Decide on the exact point where the wire is to be anchored, but don't cut it yet.
2. Rub down the place to be soldered and wipe it with a dry cloth.
3. Heat the place with the tip of the soldering iron.
4. When the place is hot enough, bring the end of the solder across to the tip of the soldering iron and allow it to melt and run down onto the wire. Don't use too much solder, because you don't want any drops or lumps to form.
5. Let it cool until the solder hardens (the surface suddenly

Frayed cables should be replaced, especially if there are broken strands between the end of the outer cable and the nipple or anchor bolt. *Soldering* is the best way to avoid such fraying (see below).

The length and direction of the outer cable is carefully calculated so that it runs as directly as possible between lever and brake or changer without forming any tight bends. This should also be the case when the handlebars are turned or the lever is activated.

The outer cable is sold by the metre at bicycle shops, where it is cut off to the exact length required. You should make sure there are no snags on the inside of the cable that would prevent the inner cable from

moving freely inside it. The plastic covering should be cut off about 6mm short of the end so that a ferrule can be screwed on over the end.

The brakes and gears can be adjusted 6 5 by changing the cable tension. There is usually a special adjustment mechanism for this 7. The brakes or gears can be made tighter by increasing the cable tension: you first loosen the adjusting nut while holding the adjusting barrel; you then unscrew the adjusting barrel and hold it in its new position while tightening up the adjusting nut again.

If the adjusting barrel can't be unscrewed any further, you should screw it right back in again, shorten the length of inner cable held by the anchor bolt 6, and then follow the loses its sheen).

6. Cut the wire to the desired length and rub down to even out any irregularities.

Preventive maintenance

Regular inspection and servicing can often avoid more serious repairs at a later stage. It is not enough to check that everything is just about in order. Cycle maintenance also involves regular cleaning, greasing and adjustment.

I personally recommend inspecting and servicing the bike at regular weekly, monthly and half-yearly intervals. Below is a list of the things to be checked at each of these regular inspections. Any consequent repair jobs are described in the corresponding sections later in the book.

Weekly service

Hand brakes

• Hold the bike with both hands on the bars. Squeeze the front brake lever ① while at the same time pushing the bike sharply forwards. When the brakes stop the wheel turning, there should be at least a 2cm gap between the lever and the bar.

• Check the back brakes in the same way, pressing down on the saddle with the other hand as you push the bike.

• If the brakes need adjusting, follow the instructions on pages 67–68.

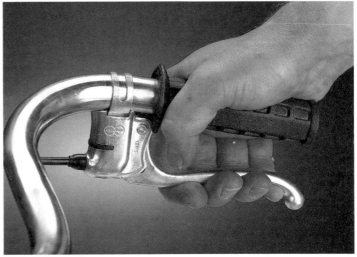

Fig. 1

Tyre pressures

• Both tyres should be *firm* and the valves should be firmly installed.

• If necessary, follow the repair procedure on pages 52–55. (It is best to have a tyre pump and repair kit with you at all times.)

Wheels

• Lift each wheel and turn it. It should turn freely, and should always come eventually to rest with the tyre valve at the bottom.

• Grip the wheel at the top near the front forks or seat stays, and try to push it to the left and to the right. It should remain firm without any play.

• If necessary, correct this according to the procedures on pages 58–59.

Handlebars and saddle

• Check that the bars are at the correct height for you and that they are straight and firm-

ly adjusted.

• Check the saddle in the same way.

• If necessary, follow the correction procedures on pages 26 and/or 31.

Gears

• Make sure that the gear lever (or levers in the case of derailleur gears) is held firmly in the correct position and moves easily and definitely between the gears.

• Check that all the gears engage properly by lifting the back wheel and switching the gear lever(s) while the wheel is turning.

• If necessary, follow the adjustment procedures on page 79 or 83.

Lights

• Engage the dynamo and turn the wheel fast so that you can check that the lights are working properly. Point the light you are checking at a light-coloured wall so that you can see any light that is reflected.

- Make sure the front light is correctly adjusted so that it shines on the ground 10m in front of the bike.
- If necessary, follow the correction procedures on pages 97–99.

Bell

- Ring the bell to check that it is loud enough, firmly fixed and easy to reach.
- If necessary, follow the instructions on pages 103.

Visual inspection

- See if there is anything else that is loose or missing or not working properly.
- Tighten, adjust, repair or replace if necessary.

Monthly service

Checking

General points

Check that all parts and screw joints are properly firm. Tighten up screw joints and replace all missing or badly damaged parts.

Bearings

Check all turning parts (wheels, bottom bracket axle, pedals, steering and gears) to see that they move freely without any play, resistance or noise. If necessary, adjust, lubricate or repair according to the instructions in the relevant sections of the book.

Brake and gear cables

Check that the Bowden cables in the brake and gear

systems work smoothly and are correctly installed. If necessary, correct, lubricate, adjust or replace according to the instructions on pages 14–15 or in the other relevant sections of the book.

Tyres

Hang the bike up or place it upside-down, and examine each tyre carefully all over to check it is in good condition. Remove any stones or gravel, and any pieces of glass or metal. Repair any further damage according to the instructions on pages 52–55. If necessary, replace the tube, the valve or the outer covering.

Wheels

Turn each wheel slowly and check that the rim isn't buckled. If it is, then the wheel should be straightened or trued according to the instructions on pages 59–61.

The track

Check that the bicycle is 'in track'. Stand behind the bike, and see if the two wheels align exactly, one in front of the other. If not, then either the frame or the forks are bent, or else one of the wheels isn't properly centred. To find out which problem it might be and the possible solution, turn to the relevant sections of the book.

Rim brakes

In addition to the weekly hand-brake test (see previous page), the brake blocks should also be checked. They should protrude at least 3mm

from the brake shoes, and both blocks should make simultaneous contact with the rim for the whole of their length. If necessary, they should be corrected according to the instructions on pages 71–72.

Chain

Check the condition of the chain. If it is dirty or squeaky, it should be removed, cleaned and lubricated according to the instructions on pages 48–49. If there are no derailleur gears, you should also check that the chain is neither too loose nor too tight. You should be able to move it about 2cm up or down in the middle.

Gears

Apart from the adjustments already mentioned, you should clean every part of the gear system and lubricate it with light oil.

Lights

Apart from the weekly check (see previous page), you should make sure that the whole dynamo system is properly adjusted according to the instructions on pages 96–99, and that all connections are in good condition.

Lubrication

Follow the lubrication instructions overleaf for all moving parts of the bicycle.

Half-yearly service

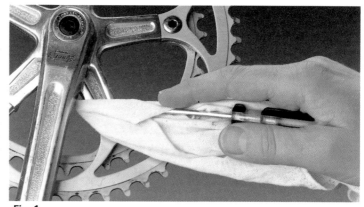

Fig. 1

If you use your bike all the year round, you should carry out an extra-thorough service in the autumn and spring. If you only use the bike in the summer, then the full service is only needed at the end of the season; a monthly-style service will be quite sufficient at the beginning of the next season.

Apart from the jobs already covered in the weekly and monthly services, the following extra jobs will also need to be done:

• Removing, cleaning and lubricating the chain, and if necessary replacing it with a new one.

• Removing, checking, lubricating and adjusting the brake and gear cables, and if necessary renewing one or more of them.

• Adjusting and lubricating all the bearings, and maybe overhauling them.

• Treating all bare metal parts with vaseline or chrome polish.

• Replacing all parts that are missing or worn out, or that simply don't work.

• Cleaning and lubricating the bike thoroughly from top to bottom.

• Repairing any damage to the paintwork according to the instructions on page 21.

Cleaning

When cleaning the bike, try to follow a systematic procedure:

1. First remove dust or loose dirt with a cloth or a brush.

2. Remove any obstinate dirt with a damp cloth. If necessary, wash the bike down using a cloth dipped in water, and dry it off immediately with a dry cloth. Prevent the water from getting into the bottom bracket, headset, wheel or pedal bearings.

3 Remove any oily dirt or grease with a solvent such as paraffin, white spirit or turpentine mixed with 5% of oil. Again, you should prevent the liquid from getting into the bearings, as it may dissolve the lubricating grease.

4. Be careful to remove dirt from awkward or hidden spots ①, such as between the chainwheels and the freewheel sprockets ②, and around the gears and brakes.

5. Using a clean cloth, rub a thin layer of vaseline over all bare metal surfaces. Then take a dry cloth and remove vaseline, oil or grease from all surfaces that come into contact with hands or clothing.

6 Turn the bike round and check it again from another angle.

Lubrication

Figure ③ shows the parts of the bicycle that must be regularly lubricated. Always remove any dirt before lubricating. The lubricant and the method will vary depending on the part to be lubricated:

Chain

Treat the chain monthly with a spray can containing a special chain lubricant. Make sure you clean the chain thoroughly beforehand (see the instructions on pages 48–49). Excess lubricant should be wiped off afterwards.

Brake and gear cables

Lubricate monthly with a spray can at the points where the inner cable protrudes from the outer cable (or passes through the guides mounted on the frame). Remove excess lubricant afterwards. When you remove or replace a cable,

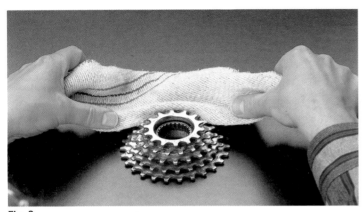

Fig. 2

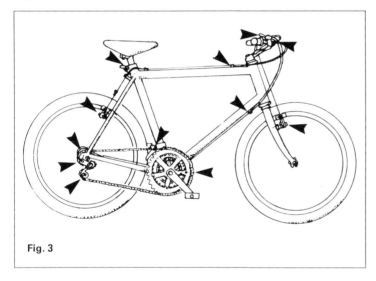

Fig. 3

articulate. Oil lightly, and remove any excess.

Bearings

Once a year these should be dismantled, cleaned and refilled with ballbearing grease.

Brake hubs

Lubricate once a year. For back-pedal brakes with a grease nipple, follow the same procedure as for gear hubs. For drum brakes or pedal brakes without a nipple, do the same as for bearings.

you should grease it with vaseline or a similar lubricant before threading it back into the outer cable.

Derailleur gears and hub-gear controls

Lubricate monthly with a spray can after a thorough clean. Concentrate on the turning points and adjusting mechanisms, and also on the sprockets that make up the freewheel **2**. Wipe off excess lubricant afterwards.

Gear hubs

Once a month put 10 drops of mineral oil (SAE 30, for example) into the grease nipple. Gear hubs without a grease nipple don't need lubricating.

Rim brakes

Lubricate monthly with a spray can after a thorough clean, but confine yourself to the control and adjustment mechanisms and the points where the levers and stirrups

Frame, steering and saddle

The frame of a bicycle is the basic skeleton to which all the other parts are attached, including the steering and the saddle. The frame itself doesn't need very much maintenance, but the saddle and steering must be continually serviced and adjusted to ensure the safety and comfort of the rider.

The frame

Touching up paintwork

Wash and dry the bike thoroughly before tackling any of the paintwork. Remove any parts attached to the sections you are about to work on, and make sure that the areas exposed are also clean and dry.

Equipment

- a cloth
- emery paper or steel wool
- a small paintbrush
- metal lacquer of the appropriate shade (usually of the kind supplied by the cycle manufacturer for repair purposes, though occasionally even the basic lacquer itself).

Procedure

1. Rub down any damaged or corroded areas until the metal shines.

2. Remove dust and shavings with a dry cloth; clean the area with white spirit or turpentine, and wipe dry.

3. Stir the lacquer thoroughly, and apply it with the tip of your paintbrush, but only to those areas where the lacquer has been removed (try to prevent it overlapping the existing paintwork) **2**.

4. Remove any excess, including drips.

5. Close the lacquer tin firmly, and store it standing upside-down.

6. Clean the paintbrush thoroughly with white spirit or turpentine, and store it with the bristles pointing upwards.

7. Allow 24 hours for the lacquer to dry.

8. If another application is needed, rub down the first layer lightly with steel wool or

Fig. 1

Fig. 2

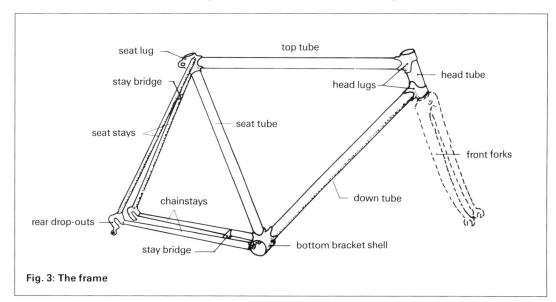

seat lug

top tube

stay bridge

head tube

head lugs

seat stays

seat tube

front forks

chainstays

down tube

rear drop-outs

stay bridge

bottom bracket shell

Fig. 3: The frame

fine emery paper, and then repeat steps 2 to 7 above.

Inspecting the frame

Always inspect the frame after a fall or a collision. Often it is not the frame itself but the front forks that are damaged (see pages 29–30).

Equipment

• a 3m length of string or thread

• a straight-edge calibrated in millimetres

• a 60cm-long metal rule.

Procedure

1. Check the points marked by arrows in Figure **1** for any visible cracks, twists, dents or bulges **2**. If the frame is badly damaged, show it to a cycle specialist to see if it is still serviceable.

2. Remove the back wheel (see page 56ff) and any attachments that will hinder your repair work.

3. Thread the string around the frame as shown in **4** and pull it tight. Measure and compare the distance of the string or thread either side of the seat tube and either side of the down tube **3**. If corresponding measurements are out by more than 1.5mm, then the frame is bent. If this is the case, show the frame to a cycle specialist, who will straighten it (or tell you if it is too badly bent to be repaired).

4. Check that the rear dropouts are straight (this is also

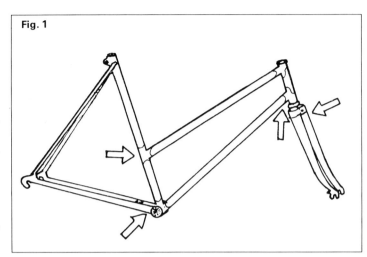

Fig. 1

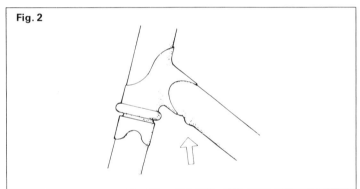

Fig. 2

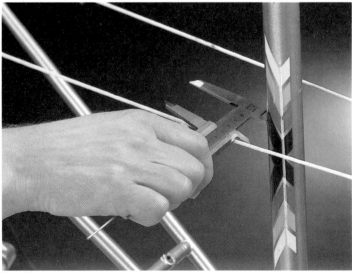

Fig. 3

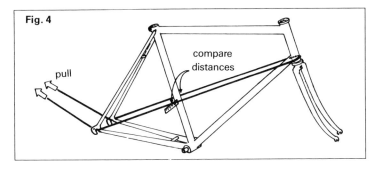

Fig. 4

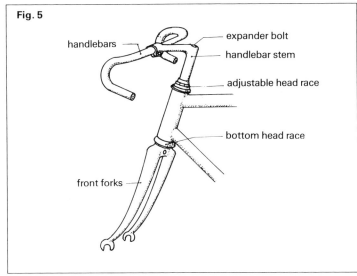

Fig. 5

handlebars — expander bolt — handlebar stem — adjustable head race — bottom head race — front forks

necessary if derailleur gears won't change properly). To do this, place the long metal rule flat against each drop-out **6**, and measure and compare the respective distances either side of the seat tube. Then add these both up together with the diameter of the seat tube, and compare the result with the distance between the rear drop-outs. If either of the corresponding pairs of distances is out by more than 1.5mm, then the rear drop-outs must be straightened by a cycle specialist.

The steering

The steering consists of two main components: the handlebars (including the handlebar stem) and the front forks **5**. The chief maintenance jobs required are servicing the headset, adjusting the handlebars, checking the individual parts, and if necessary straightening or replacing them.

Adjusting the headset

If the steering is too loose or too difficult to turn (either partially or totally), then you should first try to solve the problem by adjusting the headset.

Equipment
• a large adjustable spanner or a special headset spanner.

Procedure
1. Loosen the locknut on the

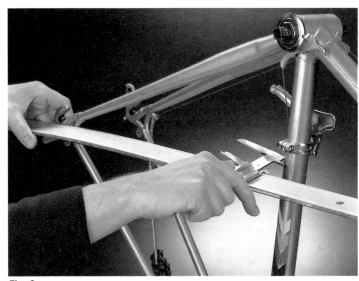

Fig. 6

top head race ①. If the locking ring and the adjusting cup are locked together by means of a toothed arrangement ②, then unscrew the locknut just enough to allow the adjusting cup to be turned.

2. Lift the locking ring and turn the adjusting cup, either tightening or loosening it, depending on whether the headset was too loose or too tight in the first place.

3. Replace the locking ring and tighten the locknut while at the same time holding on to the adjusting ring.

4. Check the steering, and if necessary make further adjustments.

If the problem can't be solved by a simple adjustment (or if another problem occurs), then the headset must be overhauled (see below) or maybe even replaced.

Overhauling the headset

If adjusting the headset doesn't do any good, then maybe the headset needs overhauling. This job should preferably be done in the course of the major half-yearly service.

The handlebar stem must be removed beforehand (see page 27), and if the bicycle is fitted with centre-pull brakes, the brake cables must also be loosened.

When replacing the whole or any part of the headset, make sure that the new component corresponds exactly to the old one. This principle also ap-

Fig. 1

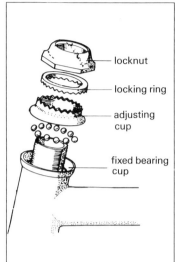

Fig. 2

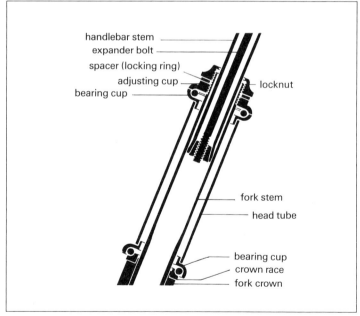

Fig. 3

plies to any other part of the steering mechanism.

Equipment

- a large adjustable spanner
- cloths
- ballbearing grease.

... and in case the bearing cups need replacing:
- a large screwdriver
- a light hammer
- a wooden block
- a 35cm-long copper or aluminium tube with an internal diameter of 30mm.

Fig. 4

Fig. 5

Fig. 6

Dismantling procedure

1. Remove the locknut.

2. Lift off the locking ring, and also in certain cases the brake cable hanger (where there are centre-pull brakes)

or the lamp bracket (on a policeman's or conventional bike).

3. Remove the adjusting cup while at the same time holding the frame and front forks together at the bottom head race.

4. Withdraw the front fork from the head tube (try to keep hold of any loose ballbearings).

5. Remove the ball cages (or loose ballbearings) from both head races ▣.

Overhaul procedure

1. Clean and inspect all the bearing components.

2. Replace the ball cages (or loose ballbearings) and any damaged or corroded cups (ie where the cup races are irregular or visibly worn). Make sure the new parts are of the same make and threading as the originals.

3. If the fixed bearing cups need replacing, remove the old ones by using a large screwdriver and tapping it with a hammer. Work all around each cup, tapping gently until it eventually comes off the head tube.

4. If the crown race has to be removed, ease it off using the screwdriver and hammer, this time working on either side where the crown race is accessible ▣.

5. To fit new bearing cups, place each one exactly straight in the head tube, put a block of wood over it as protection and gently hammer it home ▣.

6. To replace the crown race, place it exactly straight over the fork stem and place the metal tube over it; tap the tube gently with a hammer until the crown race is firmly in place.

7. Clean all components and fill the bearing cups with ballbearing grease.

Useful tips

• If the bearing cups or crown race won't fit properly, ask a specialist for a replacement that will fit. If necessary he can adapt the fork crown so that the crown race fits. With a new frame it is sometimes necessary to adjust the seatings in the head tube where the bearing cups fit.

• Before reassembly, check that the fork steerer tube is still exactly straight. If it is at all bent, it will also need to be replaced.

Assembly procedure

1. Turn the frame upside-down; place a ball cage or loose balls in the bottom head race, which is now facing upwards and filled with ballbearing grease. A ball cage should be inserted so that only the balls (and not the cage) come into contact with the cups.

2. Insert the front fork stem into the head tube; hold the forks in at the bottom head race and turn the frame over so that the top head race is facing upwards again.

3. Place a ball cage or loose balls in the top head race, again making sure that only the balls (and not the cage) come into contact with the cups ▣.

4. Screw the adjusting cup by hand onto the top end of the fork stem.

5. Replace the locking ring (and in some cases the lamp bracket or brake cable hanger); at the same time check the slot, groove or flat in the fork steerer tube and the corresponding seating of the locking ring, and similarly the teeth of the adjusting cup and locking ring (where appropriate).

6. Screw the locknut on firmly **3** while holding on to the adjusting cup.

7. Check the steering, and if necessary make further adjustments to the headset (see pages 23–24), until the steering works freely but without any play.

The handlebars

A repair manual such as this is not concerned with issues such as the correct height and angle of the bars or their distance from the saddle. But it does tell you how to adjust the bars if you need to change their position. It also tells you how to replace either the bars or the stem. But the most important regular task is to make sure that the bars are straight and firmly adjusted.

If the bars are bent – in a crash, for example – they can sometimes be straightened. Remove the tape and check for any cracks that may have occurred either in the crash or during the straightening process. If there are any cracks at all, the bars will need replacing.

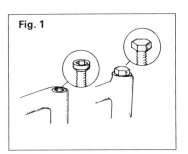
Fig. 1

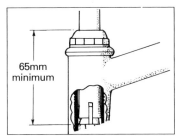
65mm minimum

Fig. 2

Adjusting the bars

All types of handlebar can be adjusted for height, but the angle can only be adjusted on non-integral bars that can be separated from the stem.

Equipment
• a spanner or allen key (depending on the type of bolt **1**)
• a hammer.

Adjusting for height
1. Loosen the expander bolt, turning it four times (see page 28 **1**).

2. Lift up the front wheels with the bars supported.

3. Hit the expander bolt sharply with a hammer to loosen the inside wedge at the bottom of the expander bolt.

4. Move the handlebar stem to the desired height, make

Fig. 3

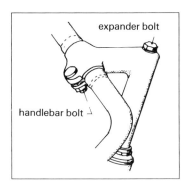
expander bolt

handlebar bolt

Fig. 4

sure the bars are straight and hold them in position while tightening the expander bolt.

Useful tips
• If the bars just need straightening, loosen the expander bolt only very slightly so that the bar height is not affected.

• For safety reasons at least 65mm of the handlebar stem must remain below the top head race **2**. If this position

Fig. 5

Fig. 6

hasn't been marked by the manufacturer, you should measure it and mark it yourself.

• If your machine is fitted with a roller lever or rod brakes, then the rod must be adjusted again afterwards (see pages 67 and 76).

Adjusting for angle

1. Loosen the handlebar bolt, turning it once ⑥.

2. Rotate the bars to the desired angle, and hold them in position while tightening the bolt again.

Useful tips

• If the stem or bars are too loose, then all you need to do is to hold them in the correct position while tightening whichever bolt is loose.

• If either of the bolts won't tighten properly, then the bars or stem must be replaced by a better-fitting model (measure the diameter of the middle section of the bars).

Changing the bars

The bars must be changed if they are bent beyond repair in a crash or are the wrong shape and size for the rider.

The instructions here apply only to handlebars that are separate from the stem. If you have integral bars, you should turn to the section below on *Changing the stem*.

Equipment

• a spanner or an allen key (depending on the type of bolt)

• a large screwdriver.

Removal procedure

1. Remove all the mountings from at least one side of the bars, including the grip or the tape; also loosen the handbrakes (see page 68).

2. Unscrew and remove the handlebar bolt ⑥.

3. Open up the collar of the stem with the screwdriver, and slide the bars out using a gentle turning action ⑤.

Replacement procedure

1. Check that the diameter of the middle section of the new bars matches that of the stem collar.

2. Open up the collar of the stem with the screwdriver, and slide the bars into place using a gentle turning action ⑤.

3. Position the bars exactly central and at the desired angle; insert the handlebar bolt and screw it tight.

Changing the stem

This procedure also applies when changing bars that are integral with the stem.

Equipment

• a spanner or an allen key (depending on the type of expander bolt)

• a hammer.

Removal procedure

1. Remove all the mountings from at least one side of the handlebars, including the grip or the tape.

2. Loosen the expander bolt, turning it four times (①
overleaf).

3. Keep the bars supported, and hit the expander bolt

Fig. 1

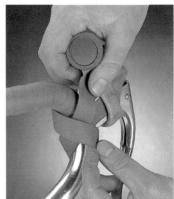

Fig. 2

sharply with the hammer to loosen the wedge inside.

4. Remove the whole handlebar structure.

5. If only the bars or the stem need replacing, separate the two according to the procedure on page 27 (*Changing the bars*).

Replacement procedure

1. This depends on the type of wedge involved **5**:

   • If the wedge is conical, position it so that the ribs fit into the slots in the handlebar stem;

   • If the wedge is cut off at an angle, then match the sloping surface to the corresponding surface at the foot of the handlebar stem.

2. Screw in the expander bolt by hand until the wedge stays in the correct position without actually gripping.

3. Grease the portion of the stem to be inserted, to prevent later rusting and seizure in the fork column.

4. Insert the handlebar stem, and hold it exactly straight at the desired height while fully tightening the expander bolt **1**.

Taping the bars

The handlebars on racing or training bikes are usually taped rather than fitted with grips. A possible alternative is a kind of foam-rubber tubing that is fitted or removed in a similar way to grips (see opposite).

There are two kinds of handlebar tape: self-adhesive cotton tape and non-adhesive plastic tape. Self-adhesive tape is wound from the middle of the bars to the ends, and non-adhesive tape from the ends to the middle. Two rolls of tape are needed – one for each side.

Before taping the bars, make sure that the brake levers are in the desired position.

Equipment

• a screwdriver

• for non-adhesive tape, waterproof sticky-tape or glue.

Removal procedure

1. First unscrew the end stops

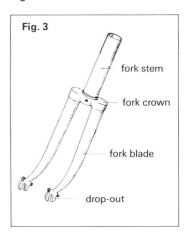

Fig. 3

fork stem

fork crown

fork blade

drop-out

4: if there is no screw, then unscrew the whole stop by hand and remove it; if there *is* a screw, then loosen it by four turns of the screwdriver **6**.

2. Find out which way round the old tape is wound, and unwind it from the end. Use turpentine or white spirit to remove any sticky bits that remain.

Taping procedure

1. Stick about 6cm of tape over each brake lever (if the bar tape is non-adhesive use sticky-tape).

2. If the tape is self-adhesive,

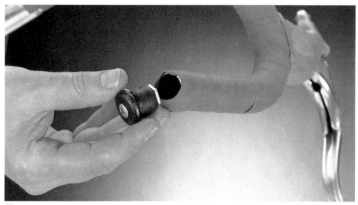

Fig. 4

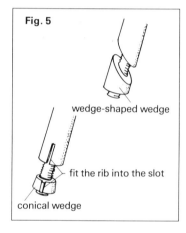

Fig. 5

wedge-shaped wedge

fit the rib into the slot

conical wedge

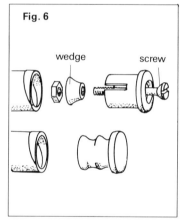

Fig. 6

wedge   screw

start about 5cm from the middle of the bars; wind the tape round the bars right to the end, overlapping by about half the width of the tape with each revolution.

3. Cross the tape over at the brake lever attachments 2, trying to keep the tape as smooth as possible. As you tape around the bends, make sure that no part of the bars is left exposed. If the tape won't reach to the end, you can either start all over again, overlapping more sparingly, or else stop at the brake lever and start with a new length of tape.

4. Turn the end of the tape over inside the end of the bar, and insert the end stop to hold it in 4 6. If the stop is fitted with a screw, you should first loosen it slightly and then screw it in tightly.

5. If the tape is non-adhesive, screw the end stop in over it to hold it in at the end, and wind it round the bars towards the middle. Stick the loose end down with about 8cm of sticky-tape, or apply glue to the last 5cm of bar tape and hold it until the glue dries.

Replacing grips

This procedure also applies to the foam-rubber tubing that is sometimes used on racing and training bikes.

First ease off the old grip using a turning action. If it refuses to come off, insert a screwdriver under the edge and pour a little washing-up liquid into the gap between the grip and the bar. If this won't work, cut the grip off.

Mount all the levers and attachments before putting the new grip on. Wash the bar thoroughly, but avoid using detergent as this makes the grip sit less firmly. Soak the grip in hot water to soften it before pushing it onto the bar. Use a turning action to help ease the grip on.

Inspecting the forks

If the bike no longer runs straight or won't steer correctly, this sometimes means the front forks are bent. To remove or reinsert the forks, follow the procedure on page 24 (*Overhauling the headset*).

If the fork stem breaks, then this is almost always due to the handlebar stem being set too high. The wedge attachment may have been positioned too near the top of the fork stem where it is weakened by the thread. In such cases a heavy blow, or perhaps a whole series of gentler knocks, is quite enough to break the fork stem. For this reason at least 65mm of the handlebar stem should be inside the head tube.

Bent forks can sometimes be straightened by a cycle specialist. If they have to be replaced, then the blades and stem of the new forks should be the same length as those on the old ones (ie they should match the frame). The threading should also match that of the headset, whether it is English, French/Italian or a special threading peculiar to that particular make.

Equipment

• a flat table or worktop
• a ruler calibrated in millimetres
• a long metal ruler
• two pieces of wood or metal of exactly the same height (5–8cm).

Checking with the forks in

Use the long ruler to check that the upper parts of the blades are exactly aligned with the head tube **3** and that the blades are not visibly bent **1**. Look out especially for crimps, creases or dents, or any cracks in the metal or paintwork. In such cases either the forks should be replaced or they should be referred to a specialist who will decide whether or not he can straighten them.

Checking with the forks out

If you still have doubts, you should remove the forks and examine them on the worktop as follows:

1. Place the forks flat on the worktop as in Figure **2**, with the crown just over the edge and resting against it so that the stem is exactly at right angles to the edge. Both blades and both drop-outs should now be touching the

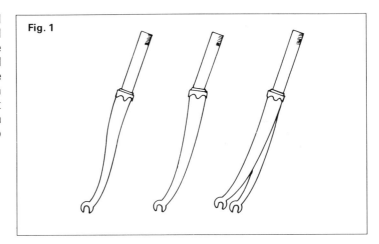

Fig. 1

Fig. 2

table at the same points.

2. The distance between the drop-outs should correspond to front hub width as measured across the locknuts.

3. Support the fork stem on two blocks of exactly the same height, with one fork blade vertically above the other (check this with a set square); measure the distance between the worktop and the lower drop-out. Turn the forks through exactly 180° so that the lower blade is on top; the distance between the worktop and the lower fork end should be exactly the same as before.

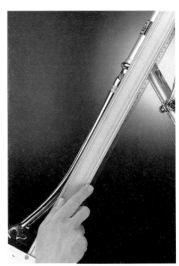

Fig. 3

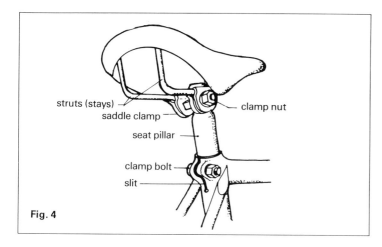

struts (stays)
saddle clamp
seat pillar
clamp nut
clamp bolt
slit

Fig. 4

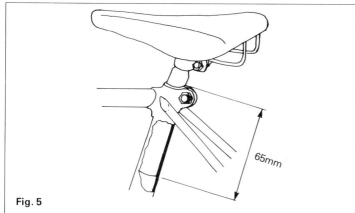

65mm

Fig. 5

Fig. 6

The saddle

The saddle is attached to the seat tube via the seat pillar **4**. The jobs to be done include adjusting for height, angle and position, looking after the saddle and changing the saddle or seat pillar.

There are two types of seat pillar: the tubular pillar with a separate saddle clamp, and the adjustable pillar made of light metal (see page 34 **1**). Saddles come in various different forms, but the only ones that require maintenance are those made of prestretched leather.

Adjusting the saddle

Working out the best saddle position is a question that goes beyond the scope of a repair manual such as this one. There is, however, a safety requirement that at least 65mm of the seat pillar must be inside the seat tube **5**. If this length hasn't been marked by the manufacturer, then you should mark it yourself before installing the seat pillar.

Equipment
• a spanner or an allen key (depending on the kind of clamp and/or seat pillar).

Adjusting for height
1. Loosen the seat clamp by turning the nut once or twice **6**. On a mountain bike just activate the quick-release **1** (overleaf).

2. Raise or lower the saddle using a turning action.

3. Hold it straight and in the correct position, and tighten the nut on the seat clamp. If the bike is fitted with centre-pull brakes, take care not to twist the cable hanger.

Adjusting for angle

• If the saddle clamp is separate from the pillar, loosen both nuts by one or two turns of the spanner **2**; tilt the saddle to the desired angle; hold it straight and tighten the clamp nuts again.

• Some adjustable pillars have two adjusting bolts located immediately below the saddle. To tilt the saddle forwards, loosen the rear bolt and tighten the front bolt. To tilt it backwards, loosen the front bolt and tighten the rear bolt **3**.

Adjusting for position

1. To move the whole saddle forwards or backwards, just loosen the nuts on the saddle clamp as above. If the seat pillar is adjustable, loosen both the adjusting bolts.

2. Move the saddle forwards or backwards to the desired position, and hold it there while tightening the saddle clamp nuts or adjusting bolts.

Fig. 1

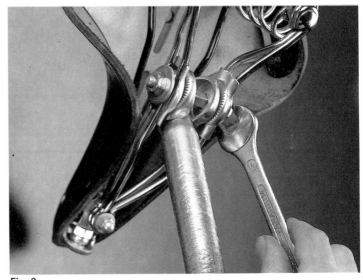

Fig. 2

Changing the saddle

Equipment

• a spanner or an allen key (depending on the kind of seat pillar).

Removal procedure

• If the saddle clamp is separate from the seat pillar, you should first loosen the clamp nuts. If the saddle clamp is to be left on the seat pillar, turn the nuts twice and disengage the saddle struts from the saddle clamp **4**.

• If the saddle clamp is to be removed as well, give the clamp nuts only one turn and remove the saddle with the clamp still attached.

• With an adjustable pillar (**2** overleaf), turn both adjusting bolts four times and twist the mountings apart to remove the saddle.

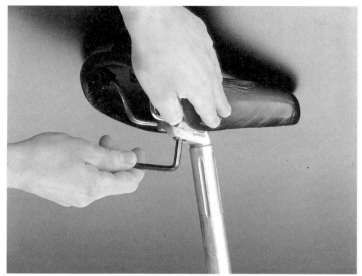

Fig. 3

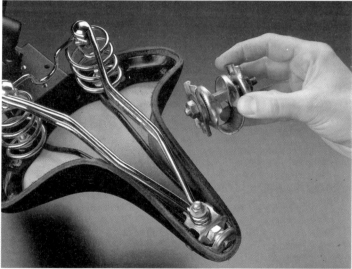

Fig. 4

Replacement procedure

1. Check that the struts on the new saddle match the attachments on the saddle clamp or adjustable seat pillar (either round, flat or double). If the seat pillar is an adjustable one, no saddle clamp will be needed **4**.

2. To mount a saddle without a clamp, slide the struts onto the saddle clamp or adjustable seat pillar, hold it in the correct position and tighten the nuts or adjusting bolts **2** **3**. To mount a saddle with a clamp attached, simply slot the clamp over the seat pillar, hold it in the right position and tighten the nuts **2**.

3. If necessary, adjust the saddle position to the rider's requirements.

Changing the seat pillar

First remove the old pillar with the saddle still attached, and only then separate the saddle from the pillar. Then, before mounting the new pillar, grease it lightly with vaseline where it is to be inserted into the frame.

To install the new pillar, you can either follow the same process in reverse (first attaching the saddle before installing the pillar), or else mount the pillar first and then the saddle. Use the instructions given on pages 31 (*Adjusting the saddle*) and 32 (*Changing the saddle*).

When buying a new seat pillar, make sure that the diameter matches the inside diameter of the seat tube. If necessary the slit in the seat lug can be enlarged using a thin, flat metal file **3**. You will then need to drill a 4mm hole at the end of the slit to prevent the metal from cracking.

You should also check that at least 65mm of the pillar is mounted inside the seat tube. If this is impracticable, you should try to find a longer pillar — or maybe the bike is simply too small for you.

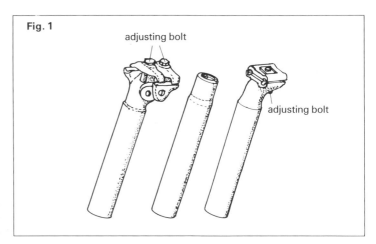

Fig. 1

adjusting bolt

adjusting bolt

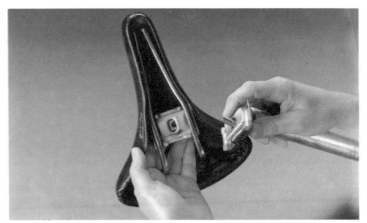

Fig. 2

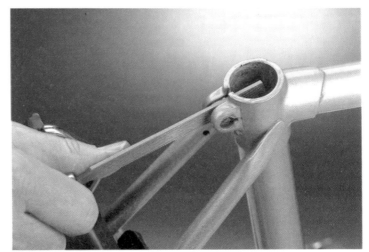

Fig. 3

Fig. 4

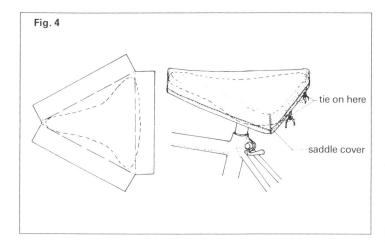

tie on here

saddle cover

Fig. 5

Care of leather saddles

A saddle made of prestretched leather must always be kept dry. When the bike is stored or transported, the saddle should be covered with a plastic bag or a saddle cover ④. If it still manages to get wet, don't sit on it until it is dry, or it will inevitably become misshapen.

In order to keep the leather supple and to a certain extent waterproof, the underside should be treated at least twice a year with a protective polish, known as saddle soap.

The leather should also be restretched twice a year to keep its shape and springiness. This can be done by tightening the adjusting nut as shown in Figure ⑤.

The transmission

By the transmission we mean those parts of the bike involved in the transmission of power from the cyclist to the back wheel. They include the bottom bracket, the cranks, the pedals, the chainwheels and the chain itself. Their maintenance is vital to the smooth running of the bicycle as a whole. Strictly speaking, the transmission also includes the rear-wheel sprocket or freewheel, but these items are dealt with later, in the chapter on gears.

The bottom bracket

If pedalling is difficult or causes popping, cracking or grinding noises in the chainwheel, then this is probably due to a fault in the bottom bracket. The problem can usually be solved by a simple adjustment. But if this proves ineffective, then the bottom bracket will need overhauling.

The two commonest kinds of bottom bracket are the Thompson bracket and the BSA bracket. In a Thompson bracket 1 the bearings are inside the bracket shell, whereas in a BSA bracket 2 they are screwed on.

One occasionally finds an old-fashioned bell bracket, which is similar to a Thompson bracket. A few very expensive bikes are fitted with sealed bearings. These can't be repaired, and must be replaced by a specialist mechanic.

The sections which follow explain how to adjust or overhaul Thompson and BSA bracket sets.

Fig. 1

Fig. 2

Thompson bracket sets

Thompson brackets are the type found on BMX and mountain bikes.

Adjustment

Equipment

• a spanner

Procedure

1. Loosen the locknut 3 by means of two clockwise turns

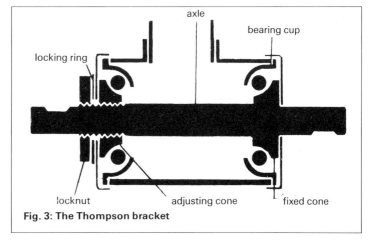

Fig. 3: The Thompson bracket

axle — bearing cup — locking ring — locknut — adjusting cone — fixed cone (for a left-handed thread) and take off the locking ring.

2. Beneath the locking ring is a dustcap that locks into two notches in the adjusting cone; turn this a little to the left or right until you find the correct adjustment **1**.

3. Hold on to the dustcap, push the locking ring on and turn the locknut anticlockwise to tighten it.

4. See if the adjustment has solved the problem. If not, you should make further adjustments or maybe even give the bearings a complete overhaul.

Overhaul

These instructions can be used not only for overhauling the bearings but also for replacing them. Before starting you must first remove the chain and the left crank (see pages 42 and 48).

Equipment

• a spanner
• a cloth
• ballbearing grease.
… and in case the bearing cups need replacing
• a hammer
• a large screwdriver
• a block of wood.

Dismantling procedure

1. Turn the locknut clockwise to remove it (left-handed thread) and lift off the locking ring.

2. Loosen the cone by pressing down on the dustcap and turning it to the right; screw the cone off by hand **3**.

3. Pull out the axle together with the right crank, gathering

Fig. 1

Fig. 2

Fig. 3

Fig. 4

up the ball cage or loose balls with the other hand as you do so.

Overhaul procedure

1. Clean and inspect the ball races of the cups and cones; replace any damaged or corroded parts, including ball cages or loose balls (check that the new parts are an exact match).

2. If the bearing cups need replacing, the old ones can be hammered out from the other end of the bottom bracket shell using the screwdriver **2**.

Reassembly procedure

1. Hammer in new bearing cups using a wooden block for protection **4**.

2. Fill the cups with ballbearing grease, and push in the loose balls or ball cages, making sure that only the balls and not the cages touch the cups and cones.

3. Push the axle with the fixed cone through from the right.

4. Screw in the adjusting cone on the left **3**.

5. Place the dustcap and the locking ring over the top, matching the tooth on the ring with the notch in the axle; screw the locknut on anticlockwise.

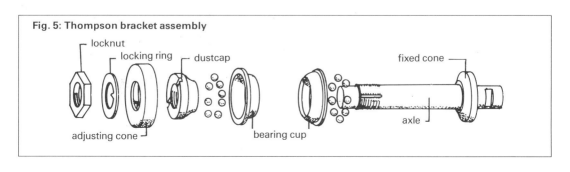

Fig. 5: Thompson bracket assembly

locknut — locking ring — dustcap — fixed cone — axle — bearing cup — adjusting cone

6. Check the adjustment, and if necessary make further adjustments as explained in the previous section. Finally tighten the locknut.

7. Check again and readjust after about 100km.

BSA bracket sets

These are found on all racing, sports and touring bikes, with either English (BSA), Italian or French threads.

Adjustment

Equipment

• specialist tools **2** (lockring spanner, peg spanner), or a hammer and punch.

Procedure

1. Loosen the locking ring to the left of the bracket by turning it once anticlockwise **5**.

2. Turn the adjusting cup either anticlockwise to loosen or clockwise to tighten.

3. Tighten the locking ring while at the same time holding on to the adjusting cup so that it doesn't turn with it **4**.

4. Check the adjustment, and if necessary make further adjustments.

Overhaul

These instructions can be used not only for overhauling the bearings but also for replacing them. The chain, the chainwheel and both cranks must be removed before starting.

Equipment

• specialist tools **2** (lockring spanner, peg spanner, special

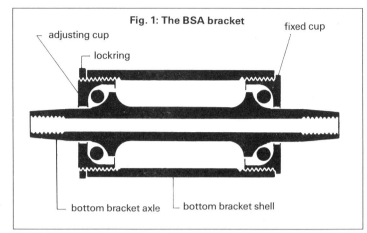

Fig. 1: The BSA bracket

adjusting cup — lockring — fixed cup — bottom bracket axle — bottom bracket shell

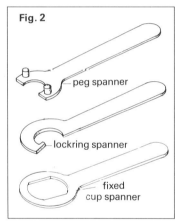

Fig. 2

peg spanner
lockring spanner
fixed cup spanner

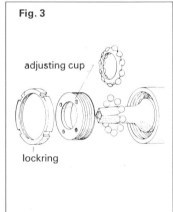

Fig. 3

adjusting cup
lockring

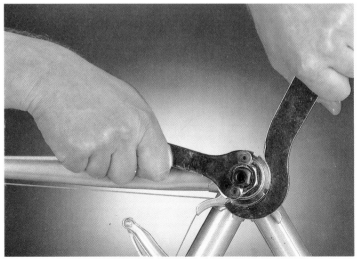

Fig. 4

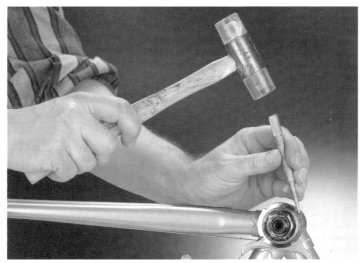

Fig. 5

Fig. 6

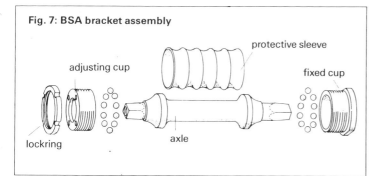

Fig. 7: BSA bracket assembly

protective sleeve

adjusting cup

fixed cup

lockring

axle

ringed spanner), or a hammer and punch

- a very large adjustable spanner
- a cloth
- ballbearing grease.

Dismantling procedure

1. Remove the locking ring to the left of the bracket by turning it anticlockwise.

2. Remove the adjusting cup by turning it anticlockwise; gather up the ball cage or loose balls from the bearings on the left side **3**.

3. Pull out the bottom bracket axle, gathering up the ball cage or loose balls from the bearings on the right side.

Overhaul procedure

1. Clean and inspect all bearing parts and the shell; replace any damaged or corroded parts, including ball cages or loose balls (check that the new parts are an exact match).

2. If the fixed cup (on the right-hand side) needs to be renewed **6**, remember that the threading specifications vary enormously (this applies both when screwing the cup in or out and when buying a replacement). There are left-threaded (English or Swiss) and right-threaded (French or Italian) cups, while some firms such as Raleigh use a special threading of their own.

Reassembly procedure

1. Clean and grease all parts.

2. If the fixed cup is being replaced, screw it in carefully (clockwise or anticlockwise, depending on the thread), and tighten firmly.

3. Fill the cups with bearing grease, and push in the loose balls or ball cages, making sure that only the balls and not the cages touch the races.

4. Place the protective sleeve in the bottom bracket shell.

5. Push the axle through the bracket shell with the longer end to the right where the chainwheel is to be mounted.

6. Carefully screw in the adjusting cup.

7. Hold on to the cup so that it won't turn, and screw the locking ring on tightly (see page 40 **4**).

8. Check the adjustment, and if necessary make further adjustments as explained in the previous section.

9. Check again and readjust after about 100km.

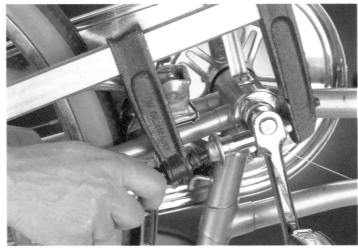

Fig. 1

The cranks

The cranks are attached to the bottom bracket axle either with or without cotter pins. If they are noticeably loose or noisy, then they need to be tightened. They can sometimes be bent in a crash, in which case they will need to be straightened by an expert, because specialist equipment is required. When working on the cranks, you will sometimes need to remove the pedals first.

Cottered cranksets

Tightening

Equipment
• a spanner

Fig. 2

• a hammer and a hard object for support, or a clamp together with a 12mm-long metal bush or a nut with an inside diameter of 10mm.

Procedure

1. Place the crank in the correct position. If a clamp is available, remove the nut and washer from the cotter pin.

2. If a clamp is available, place a metal bush or an oversize nut over the cotter thread, and press the cotter pin further in with the help of the clamp **1**.

3. If there is no clamp available, place a support under the crank and hammer the cotter pin further in **2**.

4. Screw the nut on very tight (if you have removed it, don't forget to replace the washer).

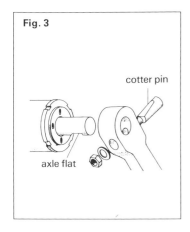

Fig. 3

cotter pin

axle flat

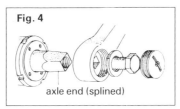

Fig. 4

axle end (splined)

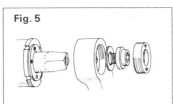

Fig. 5

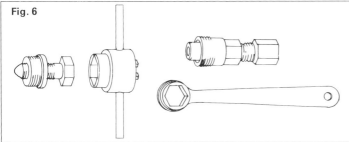

Fig. 6

Fig. 7

the clamp on the nut ▣.

3. If there is no clamp available, or the cotter pin is rammed in too tight, place a support under the crank and hammer on the nut to disengage the cotter pin ▣.

4. Remove the nut and washer and take out the cotter pin (if necessary tapping gently with hammer and punch).

5. Remove the crank by hand using a turning action.

Reassembly procedure

1. Clean out the axle end (especially the flat) and the hole in the crank, and lubricate lightly with vaseline.

2. Place the crank in the correct position: the crank with the chainwheel mountings should be on the right (chain) side and the two cranks should be at 180° to each other.

3. Insert the cotter pin on the side with the larger hole ▣.

4. Tighten the cotter pin according to the instructions on the previous page, and screw the nut (and washer) on tight.

5. Check and tighten again after about 100km.

Changing a crank

Equipment

- a spanner
- a hammer and punch
- a hammer and a hard object for support, or a clamp together with a 12mm-long metal bush or a nut with an inside diameter of 10mm.

Removal procedure

1. Unscrew the nut on the cotter pin until the thread of the pin no longer protrudes and there is a 2mm gap between the nut and the crank.

2. If a clamp is available, place a metal bush or an oversize nut over the thick end of the cotter pin, and push it out of the crank by pressing with

Cotterless cranksets

There are two common types of cotterless cranksets. One has a loose dustcap ▣, while the other is fitted with an allen screw ▣. The first type requires a special extractor tool ▣, but a 6mm or 7mm allen key is quite sufficient for the second.

Tightening

Equipment

• an allen key or a special extractor tool (depending on the make and model).

Procedure

• If the crankset has an allen screw, just screw this in tight with the allen key (see previous page **7**).

• On other models, first remove the dustcap, and then screw the nut or bolt tight with the spanner part of the extractor tool; finally screw the dustcap back on.

Fig. 1

Changing a crank

You can also use these instructions when removing one or both cranks in order to work on the bottom bracket (see pages 38 and 40).

Equipment

• an allen key or a special extractor tool, depending on the make and model.

Removal procedure

1. On models fitted with an allen screw, turn the allen screw anticlockwise. When it is loose it will hit the crank key, and a further turn will push the crank off the axle (see previous page **7**).

2. On other models remove the dustcap, and then remove the nut or bolt using the spanner part of the extractor tool.

3. Remove the washer underneath.

4. Unscrew the inside part of the extractor tool, and screw the outside part into the hole in

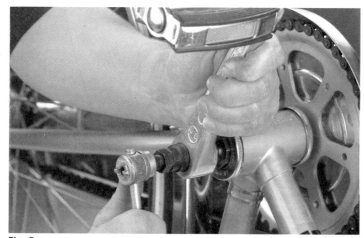

Fig. 2

the crank (at least five turns).

5. Hold on to the crank, and screw in the inside part of the extractor tool **2**; this has the effect of removing the crank from the axle. Finally unscrew the extractor tool.

Reassembly procedure

1. Clean the contact surfaces of the axle and crank hole.

2. Place the crank in the correct position: the crank with the chainwheel mountings should be on the right (chain)

side, and the two cranks should be at 180° to each other.

3. Replace the washer and the nut or bolt **1**, and tighten them up with the spanner part of the extractor tool.

4. If the model is fitted with an allen screw, just screw it tight with the allen key.

5. Screw the dustcap back on.

6. Tighten again after about 50km.

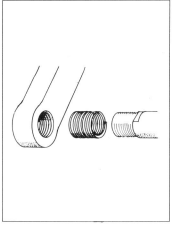

Fig. 3

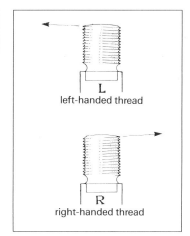

L
left-handed thread

R
right-handed thread

Fig. 4

Fig. 5

pedalling.

Changing a pedal

Equipment

• a spanner, an allen key or a special pedal spanner, depending on the type of pedal involved.

Removal procedure

1. Immobilise the crank in whatever way is most effective; you might, for example, place a long, hard object through the frame and against the crank to prevent it moving.

2. Unscrew at the spanner flats at the base of the spindle **5** (ie to the left of the right pedal and to the right of the left pedal).

Reassembly procedure

1. Check which is the left pedal and which is the right one: the right pedal is right-threaded and is mounted on the chain side of the bike; the left pedal is left-threaded (Figure **4** may be of help if the threading isn't marked on the pedal).

2. Clean the threads and lubricate lightly with vaseline.

3. Screw the right pedal onto the crank on the chain side and the left pedal onto the other side.

4. Check for tightness after about 50km.

Useful tips

• There are two main types of threading for pedals: French standard and international stan-

Useful tip

If the crank is pulled too far onto the axle (causing the chainwheel to rub against the chainstay), this means that the crank hole has become damaged. It is possible to improvise here using a spacer washer, but it is better to replace the whole crank.
If the bottom bracket is fitted with sealed bearings, the problem can be solved by adjusting their position in the bottom bracket shell either to

the left or to the right. The locking rings on either side (if there are any) should then be adjusted to compensate.

The pedals

The pedals can be left on the cranks when they are being adjusted or overhauled. They only need to be removed if they are damaged and need replacing, or if one of the spindles is bent, causing the pedal to gyrate during dard. If a new pedal won't fit properly, it is possible that the threads may be incompatible.

• If the thread inside the crank is damaged, or is different from the thread on the pedal, then it can be rebored by an expert and made usable again by means of a spiral thread insert or Helicoil (see previous page **3**).

• Some cheap pedals are made without bearings. They cannot be adjusted, and must be replaced if damaged.

Pedal adjustment

These instructions apply only to pedals with adjustable bearings.

Equipment

• pliers or a special spanner for the dustcap
• a spanner
• a small screwdriver.

Procedure

1. Remove the dustcap.

2. Turn the locknut twice to loosen it **2**.

3. Lift the locking ring.

4. Screw the cone in or out to adjust, using the screwdriver.

5. Replace the locking ring and hold the cone in position while screwing the nut tight.

6. Check the adjustment: the pedal should turn easily but without any play. If necessary make further adjustments before replacing the dustcap. If it won't adjust properly, the pedal needs overhauling.

Overhauling a pedal

These instructions apply only

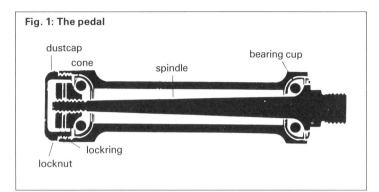

Fig. 1: The pedal

dustcap · cone · spindle · bearing cup · lockring · locknut

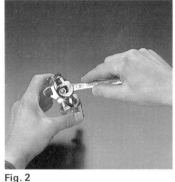

Fig. 2

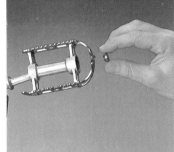

Fig. 3

Fig. 4

Fig. 5

to pedals with adjustable bearings. There is no need to remove the pedal.

Equipment

• pliers or a special spanner for the dustcap
• a spanner
• a small screwdriver

• ballbearing grease
• a cloth.

Dismantling procedure

1. Remove the dustcap and locknut **2**.

2. Lift off the locking ring and unscrew the cone.

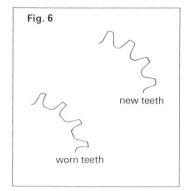

Fig. 6

new teeth

worn teeth

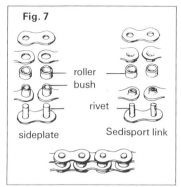

Fig. 7

roller
bush

rivet

sideplate

Sedisport link

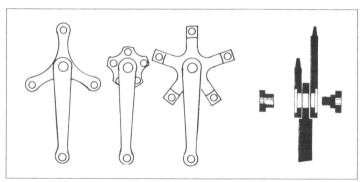

Fig. 8

Fig. 9

4. Place the pedal body on the spindle with the dustcap thread at the outer end ③, taking care not to lose any balls.

5. Screw the cone on and place the locking ring with the key in the notch in the spindle.

6. Screw the locknut tight without moving the cone (if it moves, replace the locking ring with a new one).

7. Check the adjustment, and if necessary make further adjustments.

8. Check again and readjust after about 100km.

The chainwheels

Chainwheels must be cleaned from time to time and be replaced if the teeth are twisted or badly worn ⑥.

Some chainwheels are permanently linked to the right crank, in which case both parts need to be replaced together. Other chainwheels are fixed to the crank by an arrangement similar to those shown in Figure ⑧.

If a chainwheel grates irregularly against the right chainstay, this means that the wheel part is bent. It is sometimes possible to straighten it, either by some clever hammering (while supporting another part of the chainwheel), or else by easing it straight with a wedge-shaped piece of wood jammed against the chainstay ⑤.

Individual teeth can be straightened with an adjustable spanner ⑨ after first unscrewing the chainwheel from any other chainwheels it may be attached to ④.

3. Remove the pedal body from the spindle, gathering up the balls as you do so.

Overhaul procedure

1. Clean and inspect all the components.

2. Replace all damaged components, including:

- the spindle if it is bent;
- the locking ring if the key no longer sits firmly in the notch in the spindle;
- damaged balls.

3. Fill the bearing cups with grease and push the balls in.

The chain

There are two types of chain, depending on the type of gear system used. Bikes without derailleur gears have a thick chain (½ in × ⅛ in) which is fitted with a split link. Bikes with derailleur gears have a thin chain (½ in × ³/₃₂ in) without a split link.

Wear and tear tends to cause the chain to become longer, so that it eventually needs replacing. Such wear and tear can be reduced by regular cleaning and lubrication, which helps the chain to run more smoothly. Chainwheels and sprockets also benefit from regular chain maintenance.

A chain should be replaced if its length has increased by more than about 2%. The most accurate way to check this is by removing the chain and measuring it. 50 links together should not measure any more than 65cm. You should certainly check for this if the chain can be lifted more than 3mm off the chainwheel  7 .

The length of the new chain should be calculated according to the number of links, not the length of the old chain.

Chain with split link

The chain can be removed easily for cleaning and lubrication. The split link can be coloured to make it easier to find. If you are working on a policeman's bike, you must first open up or remove the chainguard before you start (see pages 101–102).

Fig. 1

Fig. 2

Fig. 3

Equipment
- a small screwdriver
- a small pair of pliers
- a cleaning fluid such as paraffin, white spirit or turpentine with a 5% admixture of mineral oil
- a paintbrush
- a cloth
- chain lubricant.

Removal procedure

1. Snap open the clip fastening on the split link 6 and remove it.

2. Lift off the plate underneath the clip fastening.

3. Push out the inside plate of the split link, take hold of both ends of the chain and remove it.

Servicing procedure

1. Wash the chain in the cleaning fluid, using the paintbrush to get in between the links 1 .

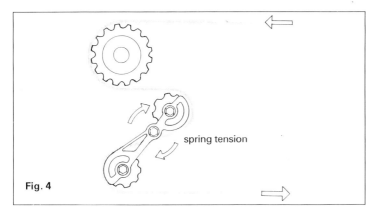

Fig. 4

spring tension

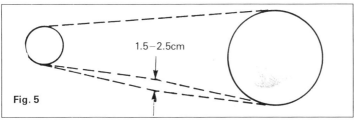

Fig. 5

1.5–2.5cm

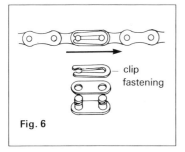

Fig. 6

clip
fastening

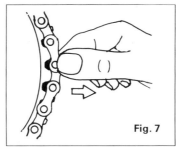

Fig. 7

5. Correct the chain tension by adjusting the position of the rear-wheel axle in the drop-outs (see page 57); it is correct if the middle part of the chain can be moved up or down by about 1–2cm.

Derailleur chain

The following instructions also apply if any chain has to be lengthened or shortened by adding or removing a link. Derailleur gears must first be set to the gear in which the chain rests on the smallest chainwheel and the smallest freewheel sprocket.

Equipment

• a special chain-riveting tool

• a cleaning fluid such as paraffin, white spirit or turpentine with a 5% admixture of mineral oil

• a paintbrush

• a cloth

• chain lubricant.

Removal procedure

1. Place the special riveting tool over a rivet **3**, and screw it on until it is just touching the rivet.

2. Hold the tool and the chain firmly, and turn the lever to push the rivet out until it only just remains in the sideplate (about six turns for a thin chain, and about seven-and-a-half turns for a thick chain).

2. Rinse the chain in a fresh supply of cleaning fluid, and wipe dry immediately.

3. Lubricate the chain (either now or after the chain has been remounted). Use a special chain lubricant, and spray between the links **2**.

Remounting procedure

1. Lay the chain around the chainwheel and rear sprocket. If it is too long or too short, a link must be added or removed (see the section on derailleur chains).

2. Insert the inside plate of the split link from left to right through the holes at the ends of the chain so as to link them together.

3. Push the outer plate onto the rivets.

4. Snap on the clip fastening with the closed end pointing in the direction of transmission **6**.

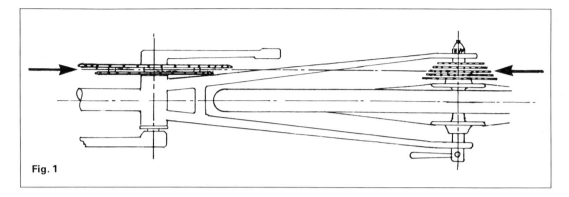

Fig. 1

3. Unscrew the tool and remove it.

4. Separate the links by a slight twisting action and remove the chain.

Servicing procedure

Follow exactly the same procedure as for the chain with the split link opposite.

Remounting procedure

1. The correct chain length can be determined by laying the chain over the largest chainwheel and sprocket, through the front changer and round the derailleur pulleys [4]; it is correct if the pulleys can be moved slightly but spring back into position. If necessary links must be added

or removed using the riveting tool.

2. Insert the loose rivet through the hole in the link at the opposite end of the chain.

3. Place the riveting tool over the rivet and carefully press it back into the link until it sticks out the same distance both sides.

4. Flex the chain a little to unstiffen the neighbouring links.

5. If a new chain is used in combination with an old sprocket, this often causes the chain to jump or slip when turning on the smallest sprocket. In such cases the sprocket or freewheel will need replacing (see pages 92 – 93).

The chainline

The transmission works most efficiently when the chainline is exact, ie when the chainwheel, the chain and the sprocket are exactly aligned [1].

With a ten-gear derailleur, the nearest approximation to this state is when the mid-point between the chainwheels is exactly aligned with the middle sprocket of the freewheel. The chainline can be adjusted by adding extra washers or spacers behind the freewheel, and in non-derailleur bikes by replacing a flat sprocket with the corresponding displaced version.

In rare cases the chainline can become distorted as a result of the frame being bent (see page 22).

The wheels

A bicycle wheel consists of a hub, a set of spokes and a rim
on which the tyre is mounted. The various maintenance jobs
are listed here according to the different parts involved.
However, there are a number of jobs involving the wheel as
a whole, such as taking a wheel out and remounting it,
straightening a bent wheel and respoking a wheel when
replacing the hub, spokes or rim.

The tyres

A conventional bicycle tyre is made up of an inner tube and a separate outer tyre. Racing bikes are an exception to this, having composite tubular or 'sew-up' tyres that are cemented to special rims; but we shall not be dealing with those here.

There are three types of tyre valve **2**. Dunlop or Woods valves can be fitted with two different kinds of inserts: tubular rubber ones, and so-called easy-pump valves. Easy-pump valves make the pumping easier, and although more easily damaged are also more easily replaced (see also page 104).

Figure **3** shows how the standard tyre measurements are determined. When buying a new tyre you should always give the standard ETRTO figure, because it is more accurate than measuring in inches. It is vital to match the tyre with the rim: the standard three-figure ETRTO number should be the same for both items (eg 622 for a 28-inch wheel). The inner tubes are more adaptable, and the same tube will do for several different sizes of tyre.

Repairing a tyre

It is often not necessary to remove a wheel to repair the tyre. In some cases this is positively to be avoided, especially on a bike fitted with rod brakes or with a hub brake system (such as a back-pedal brake) on the back wheel. All you need to do is to turn the bike upside-down.

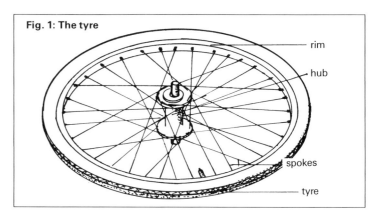

Fig. 1: The tyre

rim

hub

spokes

tyre

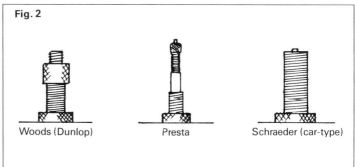

Fig. 2

Woods (Dunlop) Presta Schraeder (car-type)

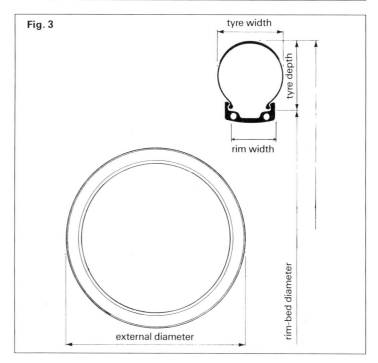

Fig. 3

tyre width

tyre depth

rim width

rim-bed diameter

external diameter

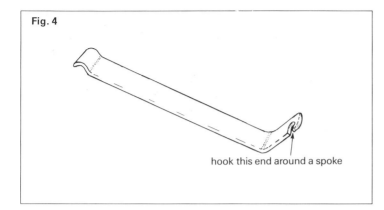

Fig. 4

hook this end around a spoke

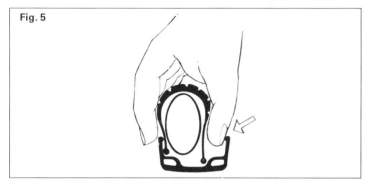

Fig. 5

Fig. 6

Equipment

- three tyre levers ④
- tyre-repair equipment (patches, rubber solution, sand paper)
- a tyre pump.

Procedure

1. Check the valve carefully, as this is often where the leak is. If necessary tighten the valve or replace the inside of it (on Woods valves maybe only the rubber insert) and reinflate the tyre.

2. If that doesn't solve the problem, you should carefully examine the whole outer surface of the tyre. Remove any foreign bodies such as thorns, nails or slivers of glass, and mark the places where you find them.

3. Let out all the remaining air; open up the valve (push the stud in on a Presta or Schraeder valve) and remove the nut.

4. Push the valve stem inside the rim and press the whole of one side of the tyre into the lower (inside) part of the rim bed ⑤. On the back wheel do this on the opposite side from the chain.

5. Push the longer end of the tyre lever under the tyre at a point directly opposite the valve, and hook the other end of it around a spoke ⑥.

6. Do the same with the other two tyre levers about 10cm either side of the first. Carefully remove the first lever and ease the tyre out over the edge of the rim.

7. Continue this operation, if necessary with the help of the tyre levers, until the whole of one side of the tyre is outside the rim ☐.

8. Starting with the valve, gradually ease out the inner tube.

9. Remount the insert if it is a Woods model, and pump up the tube.

10. Watch and listen for where the air is escaping and mark the spot. If you can't hear it escaping, look slowly and carefully along the tube, or immerse it in water so that air bubbles appear where the leak is.

11. Wipe dry if necessary; rub down an area around the leak somewhat larger than the size of the patch, and wipe with a dry cloth.

12. Apply the rubber solution thinly and evenly, and let it dry for about three minutes.

13. Remove the backing film from the patch (leave any transparent film), and press the patch firmly over the rubber solution ☐.

14. Gently inflate the tube and check for any further leaks you may have missed.

15. Inspect the inside of the tyre and the rim bed, and remove anything that may possibly damage the tube. File down any protruding spoke ends and re-cover them with rim tape.

16. Let the air out of the tube and remove the insert from a Woods valve.

17. Push the valve out through the hole in the rim

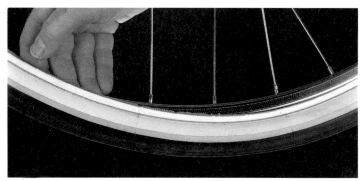

Fig. 1

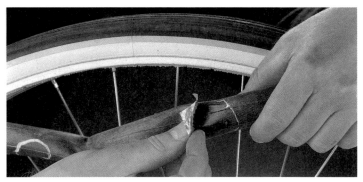

Fig. 2

Fig. 3

and screw the nut on if there is one.

18. Inflate the tube a little and push it back into the rim bed under the tyre.

19. Pull the tyre back over the rim, while at the same time pushing the side that is already inside the rim into the lower (inside) part of the rim.

This time start about 30cm either side of the valve and work away from the valve, so that 30cm either side of the valve remains outside the rim.

20. Let the air out, and start to push the last section of the tyre into the lower part of the rim, working in towards the valve ☐. Don't use a tyre lever at this stage.

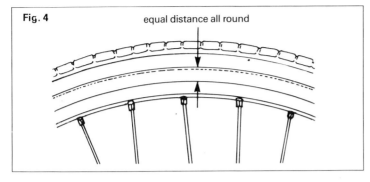

Fig. 4   equal distance all round

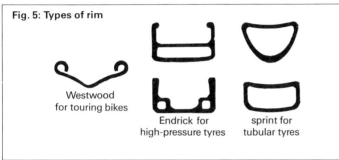

Fig. 5: Types of rim

Westwood
for touring bikes

Endrick for
high-pressure tyres

sprint for
tubular tyres

tions in the previous section. Either pull the whole tube out, or if the outer tyre needs replacing, pull the other side over the rim as well to remove the whole tyre.

If you are working on a mounted back wheel, work on the opposite side from the chain. First remove the axle nut and brake mountings on the side you are working on. Remove the tyre, tube or rim tape as far as the wheel axle. Now prise open the rear stays and pull the item to be removed through the gap between the left drop-out and the axle (there is a special tool for doing this, but it is not absolutely necessary).

21. Push the valve up inside the rim again to make sure the tyre is correctly positioned at this point, and then screw the nut back firmly into place.

22. Pump the tube up gently, wiggling the tyre to and fro, until you are sure that it is not trapping the tube and is centrally positioned in the rim (the edge of the rim should be the same distance from the ring marking all round **4**).

23. Let the air out again and finally pump the tyre up to full pressure.

24. Don't forget to correct any adjustments that have been disturbed, and to screw back any parts that have been loosened or removed.

Tyre or tube replacement

Sometimes a tyre is beyond repair. If there is a permanent leak around the valve, or the tube has been repaired several times in one place, then the whole tube must be replaced. If the outer tyre is holed or torn, it must also be replaced. A torn rim tape must similarly be renewed so that it can effectively protect the tube from being damaged by the spokes.

The wheel should normally be taken out for these jobs, but there are exceptions to this. On a policeman's bike, for example, the back wheel is very difficult to get out, and the job can be done with the wheel in.

When replacing a tyre or tube, follow the removal instruc-

The rims

A damaged rim should normally be replaced, especially where there are rim brakes. An aluminium rim is preferable to a steel one; apart from being lighter, it allows for more effective braking in wet weather. The brakes also work better if the rim is kept clean.

The size of the rim must match that of the tyre. The three-figure ETRTO number should be the same for both. The two-figure number (the diameter in inches) should be smaller for the rims than for the tyres.

The rim should have the same number of spoke holes as the hub. When replacing a rim you should follow the instructions on respoking a wheel (pages 62–65).

The hubs

The hub, being at the centre of the wheel, is the point where it is suspended in the frame. Figure **1** shows the construction of a simple form of hub, which can only be replaced by respoking the whole wheel (see pages 62–65).

What is said below applies to hubs in general. Many bikes have special hubs with built-in gears or brakes; these are dealt with separately under gears and brakes (see pages 74–77 and 79–83).

Changing a wheel

The method used will depend on how the hub is secured in the drop-outs. Some hubs are fitted with wheel nuts **3**, while others are equipped with a quick-release mechanism **4**.

Hubs with solid spindles

To remove the back wheel of a policeman's bike, you must first take off the chainguard or else open it up at the back. But in such cases you should think again before taking the wheel out. The tyre can be repaired, and sometimes even replaced, without removing the wheel.

Equipment
- a spanner
... for the back wheel
- a cloth
- a spanner.

Removal procedure
1. Make the following preparations where relevant to the wheel concerned:

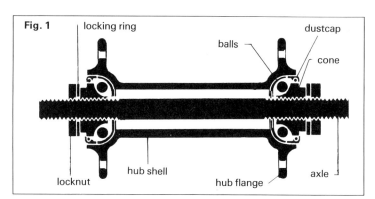

Fig. 1   locking ring   balls   dustcap   cone   hub shell   hub flange   axle   locknut

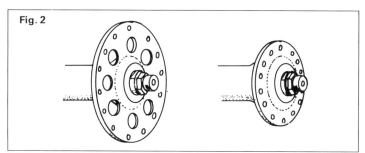

Fig. 2

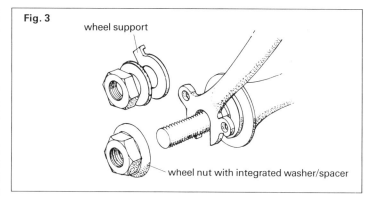

Fig. 3   wheel support   wheel nut with integrated washer/spacer

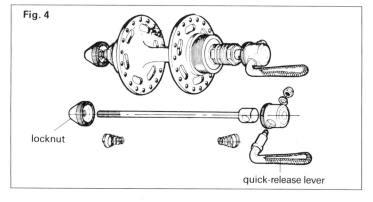

Fig. 4   locknut   quick-release lever

Fig. 5

Fig. 6

Fig. 7

• derailleur gears: set the gears so that the chain is on the smallest sprocket and chainwheel;

• hub brake: remove the brake anchorage;

• hub gears: release the gear cable connection;

• rod brakes: release the brake rods;

• drum brake: release the brake cables;

• policeman's or BMX bike: loosen the chain tensioners either side of the chain.

2. Unscrew both wheel nuts, turning them four times **5**. On a front wheel with wheel supports, unscrew the nuts sufficiently to allow the wheel supports to be released **3**.

3. In the case of a back wheel, hold the chain and push the wheel forwards until the chain can be removed.

4. Take the wheel out. If rim brakes prevent this, either loosen the brakes or let some air out of the tyre.

Remounting procedure

1. Move the wheel nuts, washers and wheel supports (if any) out to the ends of the axle without actually taking them off.

2. If there are derailleur gears, set them so that the chain can be placed on the smallest sprocket and chainwheel.

3. Push the axle into the front or rear drop-outs. If necessary, loosen rim brakes or let some air out of the tyre.

4. If it is a back wheel, place the chain over the sprocket:

• If there are derailleur gears, place the chain over the smallest sprocket, pull the derailleur back **6** and mount the chain as shown on page 49 **4**;

• On a policeman's bike, place the chain next to the sprocket and push the axle forwards before finally putting the chain over the sprocket.

5. Centre the wheel position and adjust the chain tension (see page 49).

6. Hold the wheel straight and screw the wheel nuts tight. Refix all the mountings and cables that have been loosened or removed.

Quick-release hubs

Figure **4** shows the different components of the quick-release mechanism. The springs are mounted on either side as shown. The hub can be released from or locked into the drop-outs by simply turning the lever **7**. The locknut on the left acts as an adjuster only, and must not be used for releasing or fixing the wheel. It is only to be used to make fine adjustments with the quick-release lever in the open position.

Equipment

• a cloth for the back wheel.

Removal procedure

1. Make the same initial preparations as for hubs with solid spindles.

2. Turn the quick-release lever into the open position. If this doesn't release the hub sufficiently, turn the adjuster once or twice by hand.

3. Continue as for hubs with solid spindles.

Remounting procedure

1. Set the quick-release lever in the open position.

2. Follow the same procedure as for hubs with solid spindles.

3. Adjust if necessary by

tightening or loosening the adjuster (with the lever in open position), before finally locking the quick-release.

Hub adjustment

This job can be done without removing the wheels. But first you must release the hub, either by opening the quick-release or by loosening the wheel nut on the side where the adjustment is needed.

Hubs with sealed bearings cannot be adjusted; if these cause problems, they should be taken to a specialist for an overhaul.

Equipment

• two cone spanners **2** (the sizes required will depend on the make of hub)
• an ordinary spanner.

Procedure

1. Turn the locknut **1** about once to loosen it, and release the toothed washer.

2. Turn the cone clockwise to tighten or anticlockwise to loosen **4**. When tightening, hold the cone on the other side of the hub so that it doesn't move; when loosening, hold the locknut on the other side of the hub (neither is necessary if the other side of the hub is held firmly in the drop-outs).

3. Replace the toothed washer, hold the cone so that it won't move and tighten the locknut again **3**.

4. Check that the wheel turns freely but without any play **6**. If not, make further adjust-

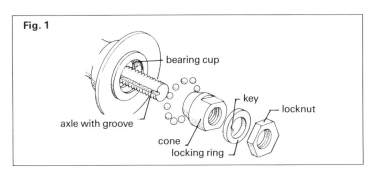

Fig. 1

bearing cup

key

locknut

axle with groove

cone

locking ring

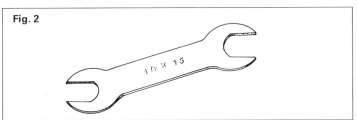

Fig. 2

Fig. 3

Fig. 4

ments. If the hub can't be adjusted properly, then it must be overhauled (see below) or replaced.

5. Finally lock the hub in the drop-out, either by tightening the wheel nut or by closing the quick-release.

Overhauling a hub

If possible a hub should be overhauled rather than being

replaced, which involves respoking the whole wheel. However, if there are no spares available for the particular hub, then replacement is the only option. Hubs with sealed bearings must be taken to a specialist for overhauling.

Before starting you must first take the wheel out (see pages 56–57).

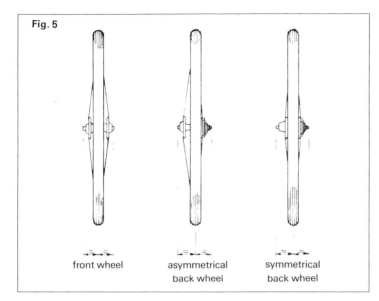

Fig. 5

front wheel

asymmetrical
back wheel

symmetrical
back wheel

Fig. 6

Fig. 7

Equipment

- two cone spanners
- an ordinary spanner
- a cloth
- a cleaning fluid such as paraffin, white spirit or turpentine with a 5% admixture of mineral oil
- ballbearing grease.

Dismantling procedure

1. Hold the cone and unscrew the locknut on one side of the hub **3**.
Lift off the toothed washer and unscrew the cone **7**.

2. Pull the axle out from the other end of the hub together with the other cone, locknut and washer; gather up the balls as you do so.

Overhaul procedure

1. Clean and inspect all components. Renew any damaged or corroded parts, including balls. The bearing cups can only be replaced by an expert. The toothed washer should be renewed if the key doesn't lock firmly in the groove in the axle.

2. Check that the axle is straight by rolling it slowly across a flat surface and watching it carefully. If it is bent, it must be replaced.

Reassembly procedure

1. Clean all the components again; fill the bearing cups with grease and push the balls back into them.

2. Push the axle back into the hub with the cone and locknut still attached, taking care not to lose any of the balls.

3. Screw on the second cone, place the washer ring over it and screw the locknut on loosely **1**.

4. Adjust the bearings (when tightening the cone, hold the cone on the other side of the hub; when loosening, hold the locknut on the other side).

5. Hold the cone and tighten the locknut **3**.

6. Make further adjustments after about 100km.

Useful tip

If the hub is only adjustable on one side (ie one of the cones is fixed), then the adjusting cone should always be on the left side of the bike.

The spokes

Straightening a wheel

Sometimes the wheels are out of alignment. They may be slightly elliptical, egg-shaped or off-centre **5** (previous page), or may even run in figures of eight. But provided the frame and forks are straight, the problem can usually be solved by adjusting the spoke tension. If any of the spokes have snapped, they should be replaced before starting this job.

Equipment

• a nipple key **1**

… and if the wheel needs dishing

• a long metal ruler

• two equal-sized blocks of wood.

Trueing the wheel

First turn the wheel slowly so that you can check carefully for any buckles. If the rim wobbles to and fro, then a sideways correction is need-ed. If the rim wobbles up and down, this means it is not pro-perly round. Use the point where the rim runs between the brakes as a point of reference. If there are no rim brakes, place a thumb or a pencil at the same point. Decide on the exact area of distortion and mark it with chalk arrows on the tyre.

Sideways correction **2**

To correct a sideways buckle, first work out which spokes are fixed to which hub flange.

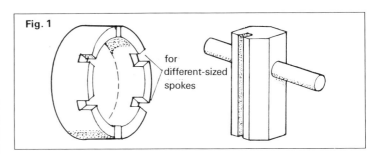

Fig. 1

for different-sized spokes

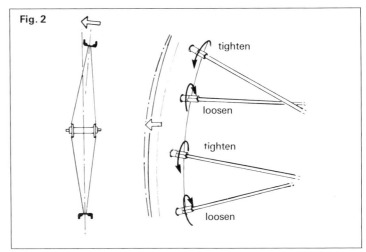

Fig. 2

tighten

loosen

tighten

loosen

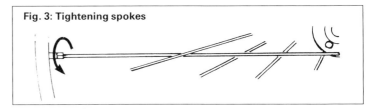

Fig. 3: Tightening spokes

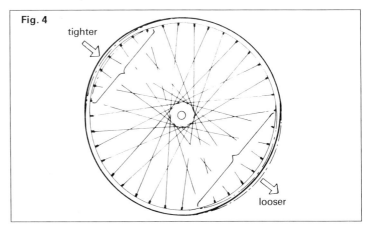

Fig. 4

tighter

looser

Fig. 5

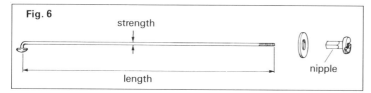

Fig. 6

strength

length

nipple

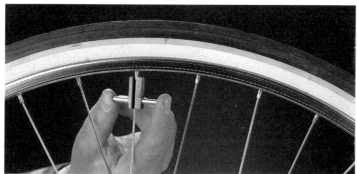

Fig. 7

Then gradually turn the nipples at the ends of the spokes along the part of the rim that is affected **7**. Loosen the spokes leading to one hub flange and tighten the spokes leading to the other **3**, depending on which way the wheel needs straightening. Turn the nipples no more than half a turn at a time, moving on from spoke to spoke and repeating afterwards where necessary. Where the rim is badly distorted, several half-turns may be needed; where it is less so, perhaps one half-turn will be enough.

Up-and-down correction **4**

Use the same step-by-step treatment, adjusting nipples only half a turn at a time. This time loosen all the nipples in areas where the rim is flattened, and tighten all the nipples in areas where it is raised. Again, the number of half-turns will depend on the degree of distortion at each individual point on the rim.

Dishing the wheel

The best way to check whether a wheel is centred (see page 59 **5**) is to take it out and measure it in the way shown in Figure **5**. Using the metal ruler and the two blocks of wood, measure and compare the height difference between the outer axle nut and the rim edges on either side of the wheel. Repeat the process at several points around the rim. The rule must be absolutely straight and the blocks must be exactly the same height. It is also possible to construct a simple wheel-dishing tool for this purpose.

To make corrections, follow the same step-by-step procedure as for correcting buckles, but this time loosen all the spokes leading to one hub flange and tighten all the spokes leading to the other. Make several passes around the wheel, adjusting only half a turn each time. The number of passes will depend on how badly off-centre the rim was in the first place.

Replacing spokes

The spokes all work together to hold the wheel in balance, so if a spoke gets broken it should be replaced as soon as possible. It is advisable, therefore, to keep a ready supply of spare spokes and nipples of the appropriate size and strength (see Figure **6**) previous page.

A new spoke can usually be inserted in the old nipple. But the nipple will need replacing too if it is damaged, or if the spoke and nipple are rusted together and won't come apart. In order to insert a new nipple, you must first remove the tyre, tube and rim tape **1**.

The more stress a spoke is subjected to, the more likely it is to break. This is especially true of the spokes on the chain side of the rear wheel. In order to replace these, you must first remove the freewheel from derailleur bikes or (frequently but not invariably) the rear sprocket from other bikes (see pages 82 and 92).

Equipment

• a nipple key
• vaseline.

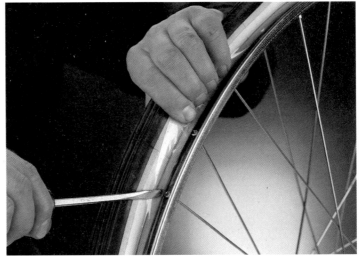

Fig. 1

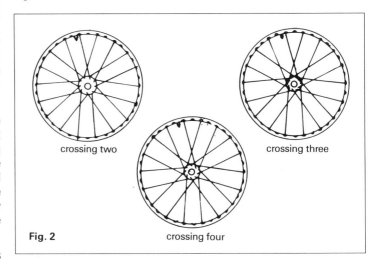

crossing two   crossing three

Fig. 2   crossing four

Procedure

1. Remove the remains of the old spoke; unscrew the outer end from the nipple, or else replace the nipple (see above).

2. Work out carefully how the spoke should be mounted. The spoke pattern is repeated with every fourth spoke. Check in particular whether the head of the spoke should lie inside or outside, in what direction the spoke runs, and how it crosses over the other spokes.

3. Dip the threaded end in vaseline and insert the spoke, copying the pattern of equivalent spokes elsewhere on the wheel (to keep the 'lacing' consistent), and placing the threaded end loosely in the nipple.

4. Tighten the nipple in the same way as for straightening the wheel (see previous page

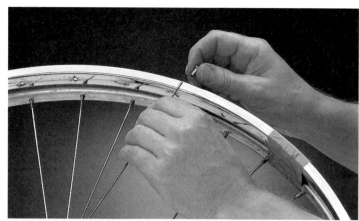

Fig. 3

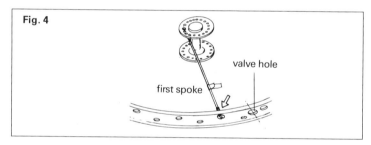

Fig. 4

valve hole

first spoke

Fig. 5

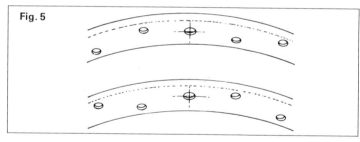

another of the same type. But the two rims must be identical and the old spokes must be capable of being reused. Lay the new rim on top of the old one with valve holes in exactly the same place, and tape them together. Now remove each spoke in turn from the old rim, grease the threaded end and insert it in the new rim **3**. Finally tighten the spokes to the correct tension and straighten the wheel.

If the spokes can't be reused or the new rim is different, then the procedure is a much longer one:

Equipment

- a nipple key
- a screwdriver
- vaseline
- a cloth.

Procedure

1. Decide what spoking pattern to adopt, either from Figure **2** or using an example of your own. Then ask a cycle specialist to recommend the correct spoke length on the basis of the spoking pattern and the type of rim and hub being used (asymmetric wheels, for example (see page 59 **5**), have different-sized spokes leading to the left and right hub flanges). Generally speaking most wheels have 36 spokes. If the spoke holes in the rims are not strengthened, extra washers under the nipples may be needed.

2. Make sure you have the correct number of spokes of the right lengths. Dip the threaded ends in vaseline and wipe off the excess.

7) until the spoke tension is the same as for the other spokes.

5. Check the wheel for straightness and correct if necessary. You may need to tighten all the spokes slightly (loose spokes are also a common cause of spoke breakages and other wheel problems).

Respoking a wheel

If the rim or hub are replaced, then the wheel will need respoking. This job is very time-consuming for the beginner, so if you are short of time you should leave it to an expert. The tyre, tube and rim tape should first be removed before the task can begin.

The procedure is very simple if you are replacing an old rim by

3. Insert spokes from the inside outwards through every second hole in one flange of the hub (the holes should if possible be countersunk on the outside).

4. Lay the rim on your table or worktop, and place the hub in the middle of it with the spoked flange uppermost.

5. Push a spoke into a nipple through the hole nearest to the valve on the upper side of the rim 5. Put a piece of sticky-tape round this spoke so that you will know which it is later on 4. Screw in the nipple, turning it about five or six times.

6. Do the same with all the other spokes already inserted in the hub, placing them in order in every fourth hole in the rim.

7. Put more spokes into all the remaining holes in the upper hub flange, but this time insert them from the outside inwards.

8. Turn the hub and rim in opposite directions until the spokes already connected to the rim run tangentially to the hub — either as in Figure 4 (previous page) or the opposite way round, depending on whether the first spoke to be inserted (shown by the sticky tape) was to the left or to the right of the valve (see previous page 5).

9. Connect the remaining spokes to the rim, placing them in the holes midway between those already occupied. The correct hole for each individual spoke will depend on the pattern you have chosen,

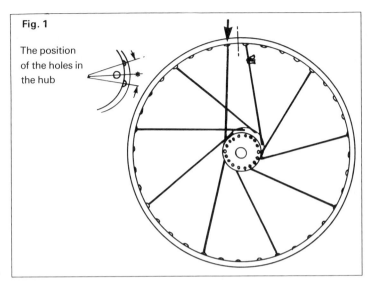

Fig. 1

The position of the holes in the hub

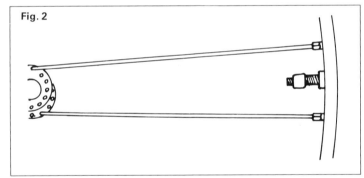

Fig. 2

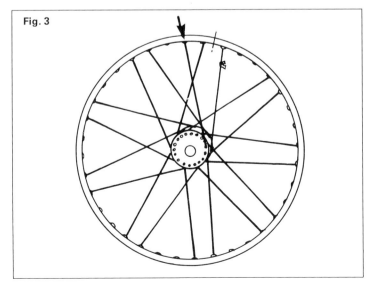

Fig. 3

Fig. 4

which is named according to the number of times each spoke crosses another one (see page 62 **2**). At the outermost crossing the spoke that started from underneath the hub flange should be the spoke that is on top.

10. Turn the wheel over.

11. Have a look at the holes in both hub flanges: the holes in the upper flange are horizontally placed midway between those in the lower flange **1**.

12. Work out whether the first spoke lies to the left or to the right of the valve hole. If it is to the left, then choose the hole in the upper hub flange immediately to the left of the lower flange hole occupied by the first spoke. If it is to the right, choose the next hole in the upper hub flange to the right.

13. Insert a spoke from the inside outwards through the hole in the upper hub that you chose in point 12 above **1**.

14. Run this spoke parallel to the first spoke and connect it to the hole immediately next

to the one occupied by the first spoke. This should create the pattern shown in Figure **2** either side of the valve.

15. Insert more spokes from the inside outwards through every second hole in the upper hub flange and connect them to the corresponding holes in the rim **3**.

16. Insert the rest of the spokes from the outside inwards through the remaining holes in the hub, and connect them to the remaining holes in the rim.

17. Check that the wheel has been spoked correctly according to the pattern chosen. Make any necessary corrections.

18. Take a screwdriver and gradually screw in all the nipples, passing around the wheel two or three times, until about 1–2mm of thread is still visible at the top of each spoke.

19. Take a nipple key and continue to screw in the nipples until all the spokes are firmly

and evenly stretched (test out some wheels at a bicycle shop to find out what the correct spoke tension feels like).

20. Straighten the wheel according to the instructions on pages 59–61.

21. Take hold of each set of four spokes between the first and second crossings (from the hub outwards), and squeeze them together a little to relieve the tension that will have built up between them while the nipples were being tightened **4**.

22. Check for any spoke ends that may be sticking up out of the rim bed (where the tube will be), and if necessary file them down.

23. Check the wheel again after about 50km, and correct anything that has come out of adjustment.

The brakes

There are two main categories of brake system: hand-operated rim brakes and hub brakes. Most bikes have rim brakes at the front, and many have them at the back too, especially racing bikes with derailleur gears. But hub brakes are also common: some 'ordinary' bikes have a back-pedal brake, while many luxury bikes are fitted with hand-operated drum brakes. This chapter deals with all the main types of brake.

Rim brakes

Figure 1 shows the four types of rim brakes with Bowden cables, of which side-pull and centre-pull are the commonest.

The chief maintenance jobs include adjusting the cables, straightening or replacing the blocks and centring the brakes. This section also explains how to replace the whole brake system or parts of it such as the levers and cables.

Adjustment

The rear brakes must be adjusted so that the wheel stops dead when they are applied at walking speed. The front brakes must be adjusted so that in the same circumstances a tiny delay occurs — just enough to allow the bike to tip forwards very slightly.

If the brakes become slack, or begin to grind, squeal or judder, then you should first clean the rim, tighten the mounting bolt or adjust the brakes. If none of these measures work, then the brakes must be overhauled or replaced.

Equipment

• none, except a spanner and pliers for point 5 overleaf.

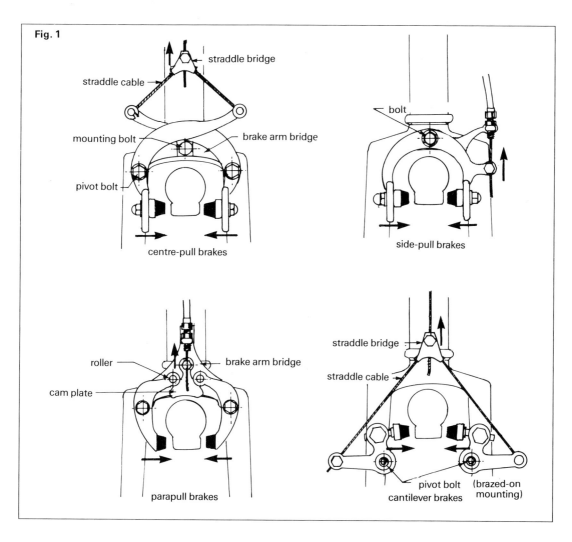

Fig. 1

straddle bridge

straddle cable

mounting bolt

brake arm bridge

pivot bolt

centre-pull brakes

bolt

side-pull brakes

roller

brake arm bridge

cam plate

parapull brakes

straddle bridge

straddle cable

pivot bolt

cantilever brakes

(brazed-on mounting)

Procedure

1. Look for the adjusting bar-rel: on side-pull and parapull brakes this is screwed directly into the caliper mechanism; on centre-pull and cantilever brakes it is linked to the cable hanger.

2. Hold the adjusting barrel 2 and loosen the adjusting nut.

3. Screw in the adjusting barrel to loosen the brakes; un-screw the adjusting barrel to tighten them.

4. Hold the adjusting barrel and screw the adjusting nut tight (against the cable hanger in the case of centre-pull and cantilever brakes).

5. If the adjusting barrel can't be adjusted any further, then screw it right back in again to loosen the brakes completely (having first opened the quick-release 1 if there is one); then loosen the anchor bolt, tighten or loosen the brake cable and fix it again in the new position.

6. Test the brakes, and if necessary make further adjustments.

Overhaul

Equipment

... depending on what needs doing:

• an ordinary spanner
• an adjustable spanner
• pliers.

Procedure

1. Tighten the mounting bolt, centring the brakes at the same time if necessary.

Fig. 1

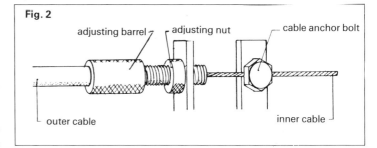

Fig. 2

adjusting barrel — adjusting nut — cable anchor bolt

outer cable — inner cable

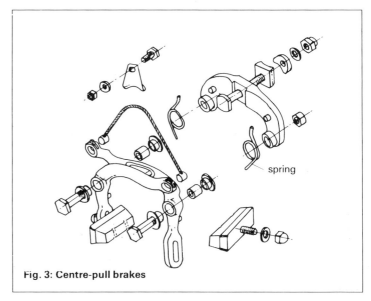

spring

Fig. 3: Centre-pull brakes

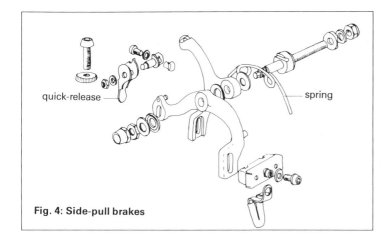

Fig. 4: Side-pull brakes

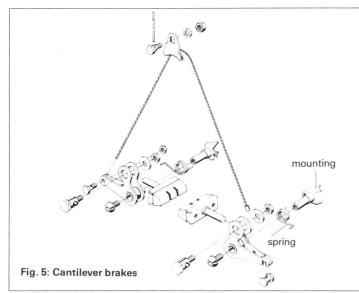

Fig. 5: Cantilever brakes

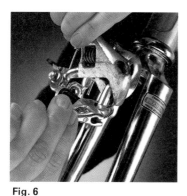

Fig. 6   Fig. 7

2. Check the inner and outer cables, and if necessary either lubricate or replace.

3. Check that the blocks rest properly against the rims for the whole of their length. Adjust if necessary by undoing the acorn nut, turning or moving the block and holding it in position while tightening the nut again (**3** overleaf).

4. Check that the spring pulls the brake arms back correctly when you let go of the brake lever. If necessary lubricate or loosen the pivot bolt(s). Centre-pull brakes have two independent pivot bolts. The pivot bolt on side-pull brakes serves as the mounting bolt too: hold the underneath nut steady and loosen the acorn nut by half a turn, then screw the nuts together again in the desired position **7**.

5. If one block only is squealing because the brakes are set skew (on side-pull brakes especially) then follow the instructions on page 72 (*Brake alignment*).

6. If juddering has bent the blocks back so that they are 'heeling in' (ie the back part touches the rims first), then the blocks should be bent forward again so that they are if anything 'toed in' (ie the front part touches first) **6**.

7. If necessary remove and dismantle the whole brake mechanism, then clean and inspect the components, lubricate or replace them and finally reassemble and remount the brakes (see pages 72–73).

8. If necessary tighten, check and adjust the quick-release.

Replacing a cable

Equipment

- a spanner
- pliers
- offset pliers (or special wire-cutters)
- cable lubricant.

Removal procedure

1. Open the quick-release if there is one. Loosen the cable anchor bolt on the brake mechanism (side-pull or parapull) or straddle bridge (centre-pull or cantilever), and pull out the brake cable (don't lose the straddle bridge and straddle cable).

2. Depress the brake lever momentarily to loosen the inner cable. Push the inner cable through the lever to dislodge the nipple from its notch **2** **6**.

3. Pull the inner cable out from the nipple end, while at the same time holding on to the outer cable.

Remounting procedure

1. Check that the new inner and outer cables are long enough and that they are not frayed, corroded or kinked.

2. Determine the correct length of outer cable required; it should run the shortest possible distance between the lever and brakes without any sharp turns and with the lever in both positions.

3. Cut the outer cable to measure; if a snag appears, bend this outwards. Remove the plastic covering for a distance of about 6mm at

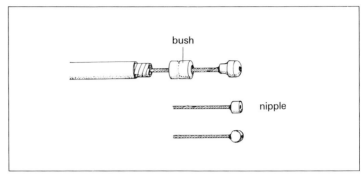

Fig. 1

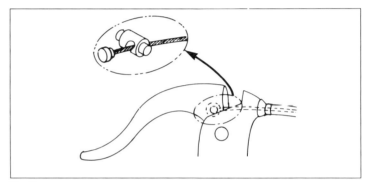

Fig. 2

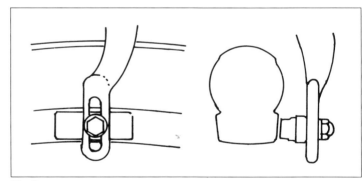

Fig. 3

either end, and mount a bush at each end (if needed) **1**.

4. Grease the inner cable and insert it through the lever, bush, outer cable and adjusting barrel (or any cable guides along the frame) as far as the cable anchor bolt on the brake mechanism (side-pull or parapull) or straddle

bridge (centre-pull or cantilever). Keep the quick-release (if there is one) in the open position.

5. Attach a nipple to the top end of the cable and insert it in the notch in the brake lever **2** **6**. Pull the inner cable taut from the bottom end, and fix this in the cable anchor bolt

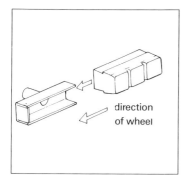

direction
of wheel

Fig. 4

Fig. 5

Fig. 6

Fig. 7

Fig. 8: Simple adjustment

Fig. 9: Multiple adjustment

5. On centre-pull and canti-lever brakes, pass the straddle cable through the straddle bridge and hook it into both brake arms **7**.

6. Adjust the cable tension and other variable factors. Close the quick-release (if there is one).

Replacing blocks

The blocks need replacing if they are badly or unevenly worn, or if they are not suitable for a particular kind of rim (some blocks, for example, work on steel rims when they are wet but not on

aluminium ones, and vice versa).

The method varies depending on the make and model. Sometimes a new block can be inserted into the old mounting, but sometimes the whole brake shoe has to be replaced.

Equipment

• a spanner (or an allen key for some models)

• a screwdriver (for changing blocks in the old mountings)

Procedure

1. Loosen the brakes (opening the quick-release if there is one).

2. Remove the nut (or bolt) and washer from the brake shoe **3** and take out the shoe.

3. If the block can be changed, push out the old block out of the open end of the mounting with the screwdriver. Push the new block in **4** and press the sides in to make it firm.

4. Place the brake shoe in the slot in the brake arm. Engage the brake lever and move the shoe into the correct position against the rim. Position the washer and nut (or bolt), and screw them on tight **8** **9**.

5. Repeat steps 2 to 4 on the other shoe.

6. Tighten up the cable and adjust the brakes.

Brake alignment

If the brakes only squeal on the one side, the problem is often cured by trueing the wheel (see pages 60–61). But sometimes the brakes themselves need straightening.

Centre-pull brakes can be straightened by hand. First loosen the mounting bolt by one turn, and tighten it up again afterwards while holding the brakes in the correct position.

With *side-pull* brakes the process is a little more involved:

Fig. 1

Equipment

• a special centring key or two ordinary spanners (depending on the make and model).

Procedure

1. Check that the mounting nut is firmly tightened.

2. Check the nut and locknut that hold the brake arms; they should work counter to each other, but at the same time allow the brake arms to move freely without play.

3. Depending on the make and model:

• either use the special centring key to adjust the brake position as required ;

• or turn the mounting nut simultaneously with one of the other nuts **2**: with the top nut to move the brakes to the left; or with the bottom nut to turn them to the right.

4. Test the brakes, and if necessary make further adjustments.

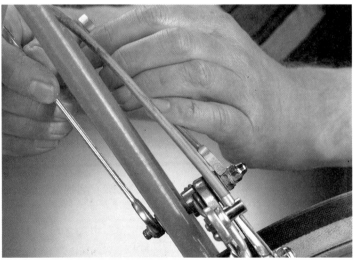

Fig. 2

Brake replacement

These instructions also apply if you have to dismantle the brakes to overhaul them.

When buying new brakes, make sure you get the correct size. The most vital measurements are the rim width and the vertical distance between the rim and the hole for the mounting bolt **5**. As regards the material, strong aluminium is preferable to light steel, as it is sturdier and more reliable.

It is possible to install new brakes of a different type from the old ones. But when changing to centre-pull or

Fig. 3: Side-pull brakes

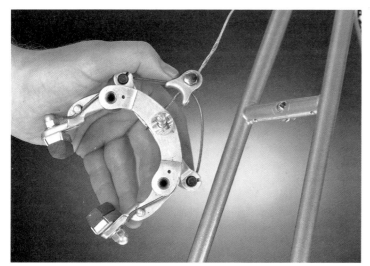

Fig. 4: Centre-pull brakes

cantilever brakes, you will need to attach a cable hanger (if there isn't one already), usually to the headset or seat bolt. Cantilever brakes also need mountings brazed onto the fork blades or seat stays.

Equipment

• a spanner

• needle-nosed pliers (for centre-pull brakes).

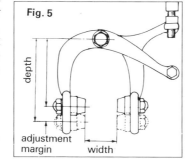

Removal procedure

1. Loosen the brake cable (using the quick-release if there is one) and remove it from the anchor bolt (see page 70).

2. Remove the nut and washers from the mounting bolt.

3. Pull out the brakes and lift off the individual parts. Note the order in which the washers were mounted in front and behind **3** **4**.

4. If necessary dismantle, clean, lubricate and overhaul the brakes, and reassemble them with the help of Figure **3**, **4** or **5** on page 68 or 69.

Remounting procedure

1. Bring together the different parts that are to be mounted on the brake side of the mounting bolt (these sometimes include the front light mounting).

2. Insert the mounting bolt; the front brakes go in front of the forks and the back brakes behind the seat stays (on Mixte and Berceau women's models they go on top of the stays that run through the frame).

3. Insert the remaining washers on the mounting bolt, and don't forget the mudguard and luggage-rack mountings.

4. Screw on the mounting nut. Hold the brakes exactly centred while tightening the mounting nut.

5. Tighten the brake cable and adjust the brakes accordingly. Adjust the blocks so that they rest correctly on the rims (see pages 70–71 **3** **8** **9**).

Replacing a lever

The instructions below apply only to models where the mounting is hidden (where the clamp and bolt protrude, only these need to be removed). The instructions can also be used when a brake lever needs overhauling, or if it needs to be taken off for some other reason such as removing the bars.

Before starting this job you should first loosen the brake cable, using the quick-release if there is one.

Equipment

• a spanner or allen key (depending on the model)

• needle-nosed pliers.

Removal procedure

1. Depress the brake lever and dislodge the nipple from its notch (see page 71 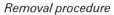). (This is not necessary if the new lever is to be remounted in the same way.)

2. Depress the lever again, exposing the bolt hidden below; turn the bolt about four times to loosen clamp **3**.

3. Carefully twist the lever off the bar with the clamp.

4. If necessary, dismantle the lever for cleaning, lubrication and overhauling; reassemble it with the help of Figure **4**.

Remounting procedure

1. Reinsert the clamp nut if necessary (a fiddly operation that is best avoided by not loosening the clamp too much in the first place).

2. Push the lever and clamp

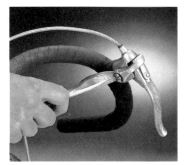

Fig. 1: Dual brake lever

Fig. 2: Mountain bike lever

Fig. 3

onto the bar (loosening the bolt if necessary) and move them into the correct position.

3. Tighten the bolt.

4. Install the cable and correct the adjustment.

5. Check the position again, and if necessary make further adjustments (turn the bolt once to loosen it, move the lever and tighten the bolt again).

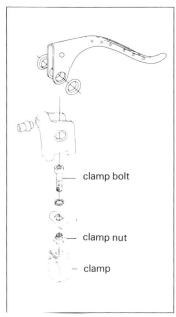

clamp bolt

clamp nut

clamp

Fig. 4

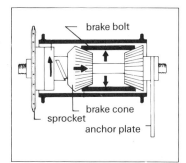

brake bolt

brake cone

sprocket

anchor plate

Fig. 5: Back-pedal brake

Hub brakes

Back-pedal brakes

The description here applies to the commonest type of back-pedal brake — the Torpedo or Comet model from Fichtel & Sachs. If your model is different, you will no doubt be able to adapt the instructions.

Fig. 6

Fig. 7

'torpedo' spanner, without the slightest indication as to what to do with it. So here is your chance to find out how it is used!

Adjusting the bearings

First look at the hub to see that it is properly fixed. Check that nothing has wrapped itself around the axle, and that the anchor plate is correctly attached to the left chainstay. The bearings can be adjusted with the wheel still in.

Equipment

• a 'torpedo' spanner
• an ordinary spanner.

Procedure

1. Unscrew the left wheel nut about two or three turns.

2. Loosen the ring nut about one turn with the torpedo spanner **6**.

3. Give the square-shaped right end of the axle about half a turn with the torpedo spanner: clockwise to loosen the bearings, anticlockwise to tighten them **7**.

4. The right wheel nut often comes loose at this stage, so tighten it again while holding the axle end with the torpedo spanner.

5. Hold the wheel steady and tighten the left ring nut followed by the wheel nut.

6. Check the adjustment, and if necessary make further corrections. If the problem persists the hub will need overhauling.

Virtually the only maintenance job required is that of adjusting the bearings. Sometimes they are too loose or too tight. If they are too tight they may produce clanking noises or cause the cranks to turn with them.

Occasionally there are transmission or brake faults that can only be dealt with by overhauling the hub; and sometimes the rear-wheel sprocket needs replacing (see page 82). If you think the hub needs overhauling, you should first try adjusting the bearings to see if that solves the problem.

Most bikes with back-pedal brakes are supplied with a special Fichtel & Sachs

Drum brakes

Drum brakes are hub brakes that can be used on both the front and back wheels. On the back wheel they can be combined with built-in three-speed hub gears or derailleur gears. They are normally fitted with flexible cables, although there are some versions with brake rods.

There are three main jobs to be done; the brake action and bearings need to be adjusted, and the whole mechanism must be overhauled once a year. An overhaul involves greasing the bearings and checking that the brake linings are in proper working order.

Adjusting the brakes

The brakes can be tested in the same way as rim brakes (see page 67). The back wheel should stop turning just before the brake lever actually touches the handlebars. The front brake action should be just sufficiently delayed for the bike to tip forward very slightly.

Check that the anchor plate is properly fixed to the front fork or chainstay, that the hub sits correctly and that the axle nuts are properly tightened.

There is usually a nipple at the end of the cable where it is linked to the brake mechanism. Hub brake cables are normally supplied with outer cable and with nipples already attached at both ends, and to the correct lengths for front and back brakes respectively.

Special instructions apply to rod brakes (see below).

Equipment
• nothing, except possibly a spanner and screwdriver.

Procedure
1. Screw back the locknut on the adjusting mechanism.

2. Unscrew the adjusting barrel until the brakes function correctly.

3. Screw in the adjusting barrel just one turn.

4. Check that the wheel turns freely with the brakes off and stops immediately the brakes are activated. If necessary make further adjustments.

5. Hold the adjusting barrel and screw the locknut tight.

Rod brakes
• The rod linkages and frame mountings must be carefully checked and the pivot points regularly lubricated.

• There is an adjusting nut at the end of the rod where the nipple would otherwise be; this should be screwed in or out as required.

• If the handlebars are repositioned, then the rod mountings will need to be readjusted accordingly. These are usually to be found next to the head tube, and can be adjusted using a spanner and a screwdriver.

Adjusting the bearings

This job can be done with the wheel still in. The bearings should be adjusted from the side on which the brakes operate **2**. If the wheel won't turn freely in spite of adjustments, then the hub needs overhauling.

Equipment
• a spanner

• a special hub spanner (a hammer and punch will do in an emergency).

Procedure
1. Unscrew the wheel nut on the side where the brakes operate, turning it two or three times.

2. Loosen the locknut about one turn.

3. Use the hub spanner (or the hammer and punch to turn the adjusting ring that is linked to the cone **2**; screw it in to tighten the bearings or screw it out to loosen them.

4. Hold the adjusting ring and screw the locknut tight.

5. Set the wheel straight and screw the wheel nut tight.

Overhaul

An overhaul is necessary for two reasons: to check that the brake linings are in full working order, and to lubricate the bearings. The wheel must be taken out to do this job.

Equipment
• a spanner
• ballbearing grease.

Dismantling procedure
1. Starting at the side where the brakes operate, unscrew the locknut and lift off the adjusting ring.

2. Remove the cone using the spanner.

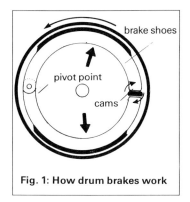

brake shoes

pivot point

cams

Fig. 1: How drum brakes work

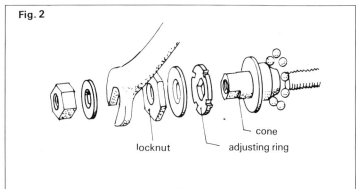

Fig. 2

locknut

adjusting ring

cone

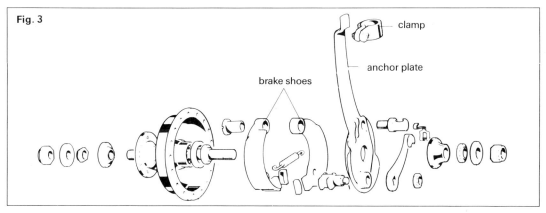

Fig. 3

clamp

anchor plate

brake shoes

3. Take out the part of the hub that includes the anchor plate, the operating lever and the brake shoes ③.

Overhaul procedure

1. Check the brake shoes, which should measure at least 3mm across. If necessary replace them. The brake linings must not come into contact with any lubricant or solvent.

2. Clean and inspect all the other parts, replacing them where necessary.

3. Lubricate all the bearing parts with ballbearing grease, and similarly the pivots and levers that operate the brake shoes.

Reassembly procedure

1. Reassemble the brakes so that they are exactly as before ③.

2. Remount the wheels, reinstall the rods or cables and refix the brake lever.

3. Hold the wheel straight and tighten the axle nut, then pull back the brake lever mounting.

4. Check the adjustment and correct if necessary.

The gears

The gears are needed in order to ride efficiently at different speeds or to tackle slopes of varying gradient. They transform the force generated by the rider into that needed to propel the bike. There are two main types of gear system: hub gears and derailleur gears. Both are included here. We first look at hub gears before going on to consider the complexities of derailleur gears.

Hub gears

Three-speed hub gears are usually controlled by means of a flexible cable running from a lever on the handlebars ②. Gear changes on most two-speed hubs involve a brief back-pedalling motion; there is one model which automatically switches to a higher gear when the hub turns above a certain speed. Five-speed hubs require a double gear lever and two gear cables.

Some hubs combine the function of both gears and brakes (either a back-pedal brake or drum brakes). All modern two-speed models incorporate a back-pedal brake. Five-speed hubs either have drum brakes or no brakes at all. Sturmey-Archer still produce some hubs with inbuilt dynamos. Fichtel & Sachs also have a model which combines both hub and derailleur gears.

The sections which follow deal primarily with the commonest forms of gear hub: three-speed hubs, with or without back-pedal brake, and five-speed hubs.

Adjusting the gears

If the individual gears will not respond correctly, then a small adjustment nearly always solves the problem.

But first check that the cable is moving freely and has not been trapped anywhere. Also make sure the cable guides are fixed firmly to the frame. And lubricate the lever, cable and hub with light oil once a month.

If the problem occurs in the middle of a ride, you can put off the adjustment until later by unscrewing the cable at the adjusting barrel. Tie up the cable and unscrew the toggle chain from the hub so that they don't get lost. You won't be able to use the gears for the time being, but you will be saved the bother of adjusting them on the spot. Then when you get home you can screw the toggle chain back in again and carry out the adjustment.

No specific equipment is required for this job.

Fichtel & Sachs three-speed hubs

1. Turn the lever to top (third) gear, place the back wheel on the ground and turn the cranks back through 180°.

2. Hold the adjusting barrel and loosen the adjusting nut ①.

3. Correct the position of the adjusting barrel until the gear cable is held straight without being under tension.

4. Lift up the back wheel and turn the cranks forward. This should automatically engage top gear. If not, make further adjustments.

5. Hold the adjusting barrel and tighten the adjusting nut.

Fig. 1

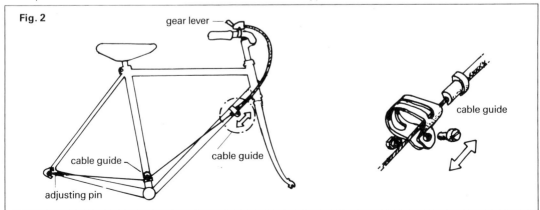

Fig. 2

gear lever

cable guide

cable guide

cable guide

adjusting pin

6. Turn the lever to bottom (first) gear. The gear cable should be under full tension in this position (there should be no 'give'.

Useful tips

• Instead of an adjusting barrel, new Fichtel & Sachs models have a connecting bush with a locking mechanism; also, the pin at the end of the toggle chain has grooves instead of a thread. In this case ignore point 2 above, and in point 3 simply turn the bush until the adjustment is correct.

• Old Fichtel & Sachs models with a neutral or 'free-wheeling' setting have a position marked for the lever between second and third gears. Hold the lever in this position and turn the adjusting barrel until the cranks can move round without turning the hub.

• If you can't find the correct adjustment, lubricate the hub, unscrew the adjusting barrel or bush and check that the toggle chain isn't screwed in too tightly (screw it tight and unscrew it about half a turn so that the chain is correctly aligned). If that doesn't solve the problem, then the hub needs overhauling.

Sturmey-Archer three-speed hubs

1. Turn the lever to normal (second) gear, and turn the cranks back through 180° (if there is a back-pedal brake, lift the back wheel to do this).

2. Look through the 'window' in the right-hand wheel nut to check that the end of the gear pin is flush with the end of the axle **1**.

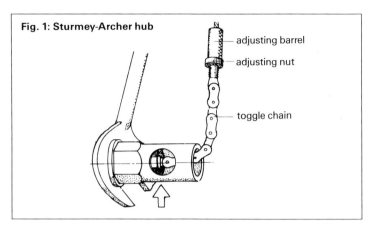

Fig. 1: Sturmey-Archer hub

adjusting barrel

adjusting nut

toggle chain

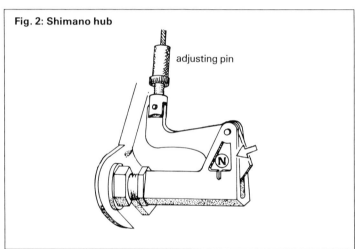

Fig. 2: Shimano hub

adjusting pin

3. If necessary, correct the position of the adjusting nut accordingly.

Shimano three-speed hubs

Instead of a chain, Shimano hubs have a lever mechanism mounted on the right-hand end of the axle **2**. But the adjustment procedure is much the same as for Sturmey-Archer hubs.

To check the adjustment, look at the 'window' in the lever mechanism; if there is an N visible (meaning 'normal' or

second gear), then the hub is correctly adjusted.

Sturmey-Archer five-speed hubs

Five-speed hubs have an additional gear mechanism on the left-hand side. On some models this is a lever mechanism similar to that on a Shimano model, except that the gear adjustment is shown by an arrow on a gauge.

1. Adjust the middle gears on the right-hand side in exactly the same way as for Sturmey-

Fig. 3

Fig. 4

Archer three-speed hubs **1**.

2. Pull back the gear lever that controls the left-hand mechanism and correct the adjustment (depending on the mechanism):

• on a model with a toggle chain, so that the pin is flush with the axle end;

• on a model with a lever mechanism, so that the arrow is at the correct position on the gauge.

Replacing a cable

The new cable should if possible be of the same length, make and model as the old one. If such a cable is not available, then you should get a longer version with a detachable nipple, or if necessary with an adaptor. An adaptor can be used to connect a cable to a hub from a different manufacturer. A detachable nipple can be reattached using a pair of pliers after the cable has been cut to the correct length.

Removal procedure

1. Unscrew the adjusting barrel or connecting bush next to the hub, but leave the toggle chain or lever mechanism as it is **4**.

2. Push the gear lever to a position just beyond first gear, and hold it there.

3. Remove the nipple at the top end of the cable, and pull the whole cable out through the cable guides.

Remounting procedure

1. Make sure that the new gear cable is of the correct length, with matching nipple, outer cable and adjusting barrel. If necessary, adjust the cable or the cable guides to match.

2. Return the gear lever to the previous position just beyond first gear.

3. Pass the gear cable through the outer cable until the nipple is correctly sited at the top. Pull the cable tight and pass it through (or over) the cable guides.

4. Fix the end with the adjusting barrel or connecting bush to the lever mechanism or the pin at the end of the toggle chain **4**.

5. Adjust according to the instructions on the preceding pages, depending on the type of hub involved. It may be necessary to loosen some of the cable guides and fix them in a different position.

Replacing a lever

The process is similar to replacing a cable in that the new lever should preferably be of the same make as the old one.

The only suitable levers for five-speed gears, apart from special five-speed levers, are the old three-speed levers made entirely of metal. They are even preferable to the special five-speed models, because they can be mounted in a sensible position on the handlebars themselves **3**, instead of on the handlebar stem.

Adjusting the hub bearings

Careful adjustment of the hub bearings should enable the wheel to turn freely without any play. It can also remove any gear or transmission problems that may occur with two-speed, three-speed or five-speed hubs.

This job can be carried out with the wheel in, but the following initial preparations must be made:

Fig. 1: Fichtel & Sachs three-speed hub with back-pedal brake

Fig. 2

Fig. 3

Fig. 4

1. Lubricate the hub (via the grease nipple) and the toggle chain or lever mechanism, using the lubricant recommended by the manufacturers (usually a special light oil).

2. Check that the gear cable is not trapped anywhere or otherwise damaged.

3. Lubricate and adjust the chain.

4. Make sure the wheel is correctly mounted and turns freely; the axle flats should prevent the axle from turning in the wheel.

Equipment

• a spanner for the wheel nuts

• special hub spanners for the locknut and adjusting nut.

Procedure

1. Unscrew the left wheel nut about two or three turns.

2. Unscrew the left about one or two turns **2**.

3. Screw the adjusting nut tight, then unscrew it about a quarter-turn.

4. Hold the adjusting nut and screw the locknut tight.

5. Screw the wheel nut tight.

6. Check the wheel for play. No more than 1–2mm of play should be visible at the rim. If the adjustment is wrong, start from point 1 again, correcting the position of the adjusting nut accordingly.

Replacing the sprocket

The size of sprocket corresponds to the number of

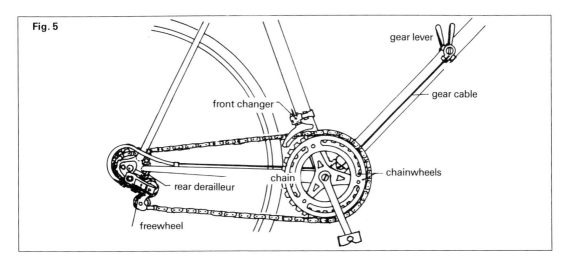

Fig. 5

gear lever

gear cable

front changer

chainwheels

chain

rear derailleur

freewheel

teeth it has, and is vital in determining the actual gears available from a gear hub. A larger sprocket makes all the gears lower, while a smaller sprocket makes them all correspondingly higher.

The gearing can sometimes be improved on other hubs such as those with a back-pedal brake, simply by changing the sprocket. A badly worn sprocket must always be replaced, and you are advised to replace the chain at the same time.

The back wheel must be taken out before carrying out this operation.

Equipment

• needle-nosed pliers

• a small screwdriver (on older models with a screwed-on sprocket, a special spanner or a hammer and punch).

Procedure

1. Lay the wheel flat with the sprocket facing upwards.

2. Hold the circlip with the pliers, lift one end out of the groove with the screwdriver, and remove it **3**.

3. Remove the spacer washer if there is one.

4. Lift off the sprocket **4**.

5. Clean all parts and change the sprocket.

6. Install the sprocket and spacer washer. If the sprocket is asymmetric, place it with the teeth on the inside or outside depending on the chainline.

7. Push the circlip into the groove until it holds firm.

Derailleur gears

Derailleur gear systems involve two important mechanisms that move the chain. The rear changer or derailleur switches the chain between the sprockets of the freewheel

that is mounted on the rear hub. The front changer moves the chain between chainwheels of different sizes attached to the right crank **5**.

A ten-speed system is the commonest, with two chainwheels and five sprockets. A five-speed system has only one chainwheel, and so no front changer. A fifteen-speed has three chainwheels. If there are six sprockets the number of gears available is six twelve or eighteen, depending on the number of chainwheels.

The gears are controlled by two levers. These are usually mounted either side of the down tube, but may be attached to the handlebars.

The levers are connected to the gear mechanisms by flexible cables, which run through cable guides mounted along the frame. If the levers are mounted on the bars, then the top section of each cable runs through an outer cable consisting of a metal spiral.

Adjusting the changers

Many problems with derailleur systems can be solved by adjusting the changers. All the various components must be regularly cleaned and lubricated, and the same applies to cables, chain and freewheel.

If the chain slips off over the smallest or largest sprocket or chainwheel, or refuses to move into certain combinations, then the offending changer must be adjusted.

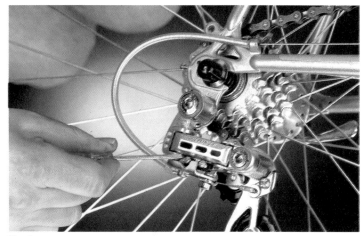

Fig. 1

The job can best be done with the bike hanging or placed upside-down. When turning the bike over, make sure that none of the mountings on the handlebars get trapped or damaged.

Equipment

• a small screwdriver

• a cloth (if the chain has come off).

Procedure

1. If necessary remount the chain, moving the gear lever(s) to the corresponding position(s).

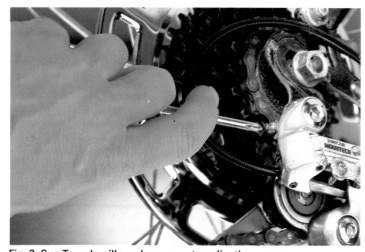

Fig. 2: Sun Tour derailleurs have an extra adjusting screw

2. Work out where the problem lies. Is it at the back or the front? Is the chain being moved too far to the left (inwards) or to the right (outwards)?

3. Every changer is fitted with two adjusting screws, though the position of these varies depending on the make and model. Both screws are fitted with a spiral spring under the screw head, which is supposed to prevent the mechanism

from coming out of adjustment as a result of vibrations. One screw stops the changer moving too far left (inwards); the other one limits any movement right (outwards) [1].

4. The adjusting screws are often marked H for the highest gear and L for the lowest gear. If not, you will need to work out which is which; move the gear lever to see which way the changer moves and which screw comes into play.

5. Now turn the appropriate screw, either inwards so that chain is moved less far (if it is moving too far), or outwards so that it is moved further (if it isn't moving far enough).

6. Try out all gear combinations. If necessary, make further adjustments until all the gears respond correctly.

7. If the gear cable is too loose or too tight, then adjust this as well (see opposite).

Fig. 3

Fig. 4

Useful tip

Sun Tour derailleurs have an extra (third) screw **2** that limits the movement of the changer about its mountings. It sometimes helps to screw this in or out about 1–3 turns.

Adjusting a cable

If a gear cable is too loose or too tight, then it will need to be adjusted accordingly. But if it is frayed or otherwise damaged, then replace it (see instructions overleaf).

Equipment

• a spanner.

Procedure

1. First adjust the gears as best you can (see preceding section).

2. Set the gears so that the chain is running over the smallest chainwheel and sprocket.

3. If there is an adjusting barrel **3**, hold this and unscrew the locknut; then screw the adjusting barrel either in or out to adjust, and hold it in place while tightening the locknut again.

4. If there is no adjusting barrel, or the adjusting barrel can't be moved far enough, then turn your attention to the cable anchor nut or bolt (depending on the model). Unscrew it one or two turns, move the cable up or down (to loosen or tighten it), and screw the cable anchorage tight again **4**.

5. Try out all the gears, and if necessary make further adjustments.

8. If adjustment doesn't solve the problem, check the following points:

• if the cable is frayed, replace it;

• if there is an outer cable and it is buckled, replace it;

• make sure that the cable guides and the lever and changer mountings are all screwed firmly in place;

• make sure that the clamp screw on the gear lever is properly tightened, so that the lever doesn't inadvertently slip or come loose;

• check the bottom bracket and chainwheel mountings for play, and if necessary adjust or tighten them.

9. If the gears still won't change properly, overhaul the offending changer, and check that the right-hand drop-out is straight.

Replacing a cable

A cable must always be replaced if it is frayed or otherwise damaged. These instructions also apply when an outer cable needs to be replaced.

Equipment

• a spanner.

Removal procedure

1. Set the gears so that the changer concerned is in the position of least tension. At the back this is always when the chain is on the smallest sprocket. At the front it is usually when the chain is on the smaller chainwheel, but this varies according to the model.

2. Unscrew the cable anchor bolt or nut (depending on the model) about two or three turns.

3. Remove the cable from its anchorage, and pull it out through the cable guides and outer cable (if any) from the lever end.

4. Push the cable out through the lever to dislodge the nipple; then, holding the nipple, pull the whole cable out of the lever.

Mounting procedure

1. Make sure the new cable has the same type of nipple **3** and is of the same length as the old one.

2. Grease the cable with vaseline or another appropriate lubricant.

3. Push the cable through the lever, and pull it through until the nipple is firmly seated.

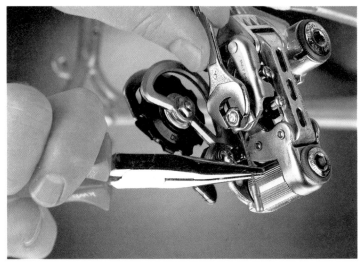

Fig. 1

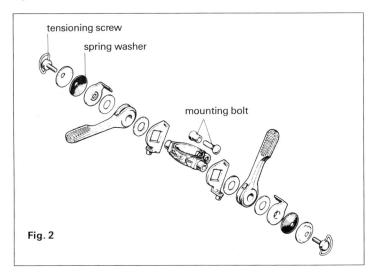

tensioning screw

spring washer

mounting bolt

Fig. 2

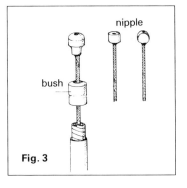

nipple

bush

Fig. 3

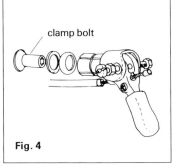

clamp bolt

Fig. 4

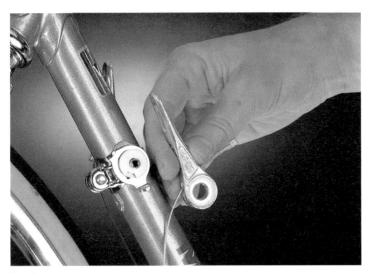

Fig. 5

Fig. 6

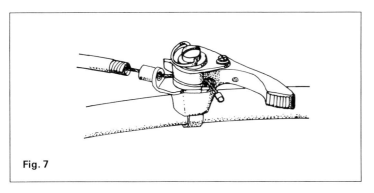

Fig. 7

4. Insert the cable through the outer cable (if any) and cable guides, and push the end through the cable anchorage.

5. Place the lever in the correct gear for the wheel that the chain is on (see above), and hold the cable with the minimum tension required to keep it taut.

6. Keep the cable in this position while tightening the cable anchor bolt (or nut) **1**.

7. Try out all the gears, and if necessary make adjustments.

Replacing a lever

The cable must first be removed and afterwards remounted according to the instructions in the preceding section **5** **7**.

The gear-lever mountings vary from model to model. Sometimes the levers are attached by a clamp to the down tube **2** or handlebars **6**, but sometimes they are screwed onto fittings mounted on the frame **5**. If possible choose a lever of the the same make as the changer, because then all the components will match.

Some levers are mounted at the ends of the bars in place of end stops. In such cases the outer cable should be bound inside the bar tape. The lever is held in place by a clamp bolt inside the bar cavity **4**. In order to reach this, you must first remove the transverse bolt that acts as the lever pivot. The clamp bolt can then be loosened or tightened with an allen key.

Replacing or overhauling the derailleur

The rear derailleur is fixed either directly to a threaded lug on the right drop-out or (if there is no such lug) by means of a mounting bracket ① ⑥. This is usually supplied with the derailleur and should be mounted in the appropriate slot on the outside of the right drop-out (after first removing the wheel).

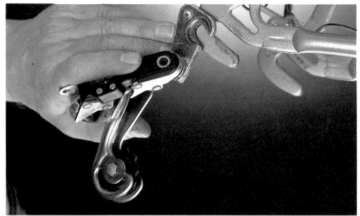

Fig. 1

When changing the derailleur, you should if possible install a new model of the same make as the old one, or if not replace the gear lever at the same time so that the two are compatible.

If there is a large size difference between the sprockets, the derailleur should have a sufficient capacity to take up the spare chain. Ask for your dealer's advice on this.

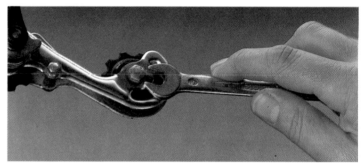

Fig. 2

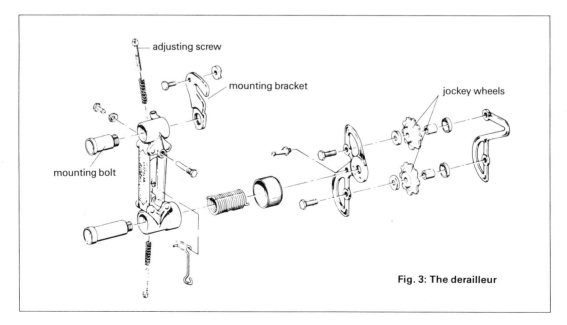

adjusting screw

mounting bracket

jockey wheels

mounting bolt

Fig. 3: The derailleur

Fig. 4

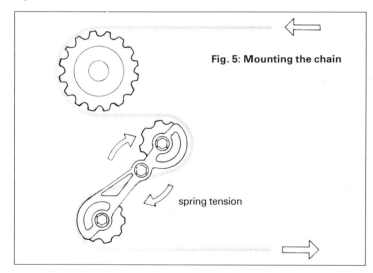

Fig. 5: Mounting the chain

spring tension

Fig. 6

mounting bracket

lug with one stop

lug with two stops

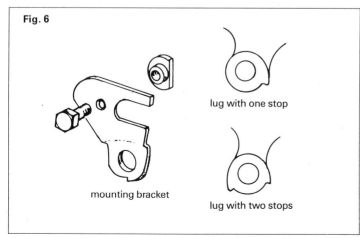

If the drop-out has a lug for the derailleur, the drop-out and derailleur should again be preferably of the same make. The back wheel need be taken out only if you need to remove or install a mounting bracket.

Equipment

- an allen key
- a spanner.

Removal procedure

1. Loosen the cable anchor bolt and remove the gear cable from it (see *Removal procedure* on page 86).

2. Take the chain apart (see page 49), or unscrew one of the pulley bolts **2** to free the chain from the mechanism.

3. If there is no mounting bracket, turn the mounting bolt anticlockwise with the allen key until the derailleur comes off.

Overhaul procedure

1. Remove both jockey wheels **4** and clean them or replace them if worn. Lubricate the bearings.

2. Clean and inspect all the other components, lubricating them with light oil.

3. If the chain hasn't been removed, remount only one of the jockey wheels; otherwise remount both. Check that they will turn freely.

Remounting procedure

1. Remove any cardboard washers from the new derailleur.

2. If necessary connect a new mounting bracket to the derailleur **1** (overleaf).

3. Remount the derailleur (with or without the mounting bracket) in the correct position on the right drop-out, screwing it on firmly ②.

4. Check that the derailleur swivels freely on the bolt.

5. Either remount the chain according to Figure ⑤ on page 89, or else replace the second jockey wheel. (On many Sachs-Huret models, the chain can be mounted in either of two positions, each of which is marked with a number; if the number of teeth on the largest sprocket is greater than the number given for the inner position, then the chain should be mounted in the outer position.)

Fig. 1

6. Remount the gear cable loosely in the cable anchorage, adjust it and screw it in tightly. Cut it off about 3cm below the cable anchor bolt.

7. Try out all the gears, and if necessary make further adjustments.

Replacing the front changer

Fig. 2

The front changer should if possible be of the same make as the corresponding gear lever. If the inside and outside chainwheels differ by more than fourteen teeth, then a special type of changer is needed and you should ask your dealer for advice.

If the frame is fitted with special front-changer mountings, these must be compatible with the changer itself.

Either· you can remove the chain beforehand and re-

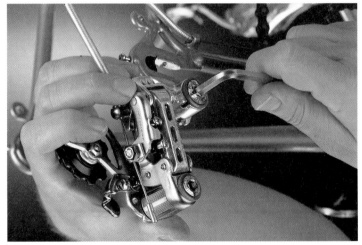

Fig. 3

Fig. 4

mount it afterwards, or alternatively you can unbolt the bottom end of the chain guide so that it can be mounted over the chain **3**.

Equipment

- a spanner
- a screwdriver.

Removal procedure

1. Loosen the cable anchor bolt and remove the gear cable.

2. If the chain is still mounted, unscrew the bolt at the bottom end of the chain guide and remove the bush.

3. Unscrew the mounting bolt and remove changer **4**.

Remounting procedure

1. Fix the changer loosely to the seat tube and/or front-changer mounting.

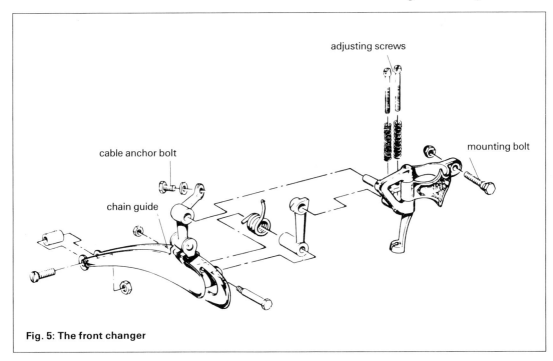

adjusting screws

mounting bolt

cable anchor bolt

chain guide

Fig. 5: The front changer

2. Either remount the chain so that it runs through the chain guide, or screw back the bush and bolt at the bottom end of the chain guide so that the chain runs through it.

3. Adjust the position of the changer to the correct height, with the chain guide 2-4mm above the largest chainwheel and parallel to it **1**; tighten the mounting bolt.

4. Remount and adjust the cable in the cable anchor bolt.

5. Try out all the gears and adjust the changer accordingly.

Changing the freewheel

The freewheel must be replaced if the mechanism goes wrong or the individual sprockets become worn. It is difficult to tell if only one sprocket is worn (usually the smallest one). The most distinctive sign is when the chain 'jumps' as the bike comes up to speed.

Sometimes the freewheel needs to be changed in order to modify the gearing. You may, for instance, need wider-spaced gears for riding over mountains. When buying a new freewheel, make sure the threading is the same as on the hub (English, French or Italian).

Provided the freewheel mechanism is in order, then sprockets can sometimes be changed individually. But this depends on the model, and is very much a job for the expert.

If the mechanism has become loose so that the freewheel

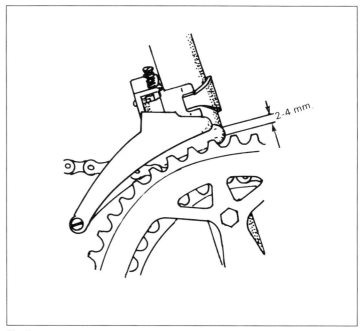

Fig. 1

Fig. 2

Fig. 3

'floats' as it turns, then the bearings can be adjusted according to the instructions in the next section. Both jobs should be done with the wheel taken out.

If the freewheel no longer turns freely, then it should be lubricated as shown in Figure **3**.

Equipment

• a special freewheel extractor tool (depending on the make of freewheel)

• a workbench with a vice (or in emergency a large adjustable spanner)

• a cloth

• vaseline.

Removal procedure

1. Open the quick-release or remove the wheel nut.

2. Mount the freewheel extractor tool in the corresponding holes in the freewheel **2**. With some models the locknut on the hub bearings has to be removed in order to do this.

3. Remount the wheel nut or quick-release to allow for little or no play.

4. If you have a vice, turn the wheel over and clamp the freewheel extractor in the vice. If there is no vice available, hold the wheel very firmly (eg with your body weight pressing on it in the corner of a room) and attach the adjustable spanner.

5. Turn the wheel or extractor tool once anticlockwise to loosen it; unscrew the wheel nut or quick-release by one turn, and continue to unscrew the wheel or extractor tool until the freewheel can be removed by hand.

Remounting procedure

1. Thoroughly clean the threads of the freewheel and hub, and lightly grease them.

2. Place a spacer ring over the hub if this is needed to keep the freewheel away from the spokes.

3. Carefully place the freewheel over the thread on the hub and screw it on by hand. It will screw tight automatically when the bike is next ridden.

4. Try out the gears and make adjustments accordingly.

Adjusting the freewheel bearings

It is not always necessary to detach the freewheel for this job. If a ring with two holes in it (the adjusting cone) is visible on the outside of the freewheel, it can be left on the wheel. If not the freewheel must first be removed, as in this case the adjusting cone must be on the inside of the freewheel. The job must always be done with the wheel taken out.

Equipment

• a peg spanner or a hammer and punch

• a cloth

• ballbearing grease.

Procedure

1. Turn the wheel or freewheel so that the adjusting cone lies uppermost and hold it firm.

2. Using the peg spanner or hammer and punch, turn the

adjusting cone clockwise to remove it (left-handed thread) . (The freewheel in the picture is unusual in having a right-handed thread).

3. If the bearings were too loose, remove a spacer ring.

4. Fill the ball race with ballbearing grease, taking care not to lose any of the balls.

5. Screw the adjusting cone back on again, turning it anti-clockwise to tighten it.

6. Try out the freewheel, and if necessary make further adjustments, adding or removing a spacer ring as appropriate.

Fig. 1

Lights and accessories

This chapter deals with all the parts of the bike that are not directly involved in its propulsion. They range from items that are legally required, such as the lights and the bell, to optional items that may or may not be useful, such as mudguards or a lollipop reflector. The first section gives detailed consideration to the lighting system, which is vitally important. There follows a more general account of the jobs that need doing to the other accessories.

The lighting system

A dynamo lighting system is legally required in some countries (though not in Britain). Repairing and maintaining the lights is especially vital to road safety, because faults in the lighting system lead to more accidents than any other type of fault.

A dynamo system consists of a dynamo and a front and back light. The electric current produced by the dynamo flows through insulated wires to the front and back lights, and returns to the dynamo via the metal of the frame. Figure 1 shows how the different parts are connected together.

The dynamo should be positioned so that it remains 5–8mm away from the tyre while not in use, but rests firmly flat against the tyre when engaged. The dynamo axle should run in a straight line from the wheel axle 2. The angle can be adjusted by lossening the mounting bolt, pushing or turning the mounting plate and retightening the bolt 3.

The front light should be positioned so that the main light beam hits the ground about 10–15m directly in front of the bicycle. The mountings should be screwed sufficiently tight not to move 5, but at the same time with enough play so that small adjustments can be made by hand. The front light should be positioned as high as possible so as to illuminate the largest possible area in front of the bike.

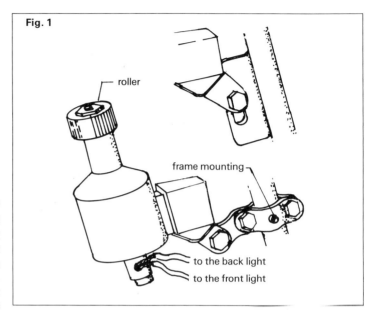
Fig. 1

roller

frame mounting

to the back light

to the front light

Fig. 2

Fig. 3

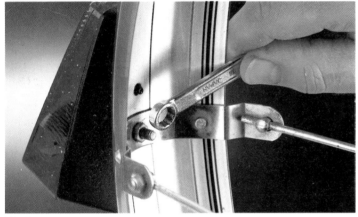
Fig. 4

Fig. 5

The back light is mounted on the rear mudguard or right seat stay. It must be positioned so that the beam is directed back horizontally in line with the bike. If it is mounted on the seat stay, the beam must not be obscured by the luggage rack.

In a dynamo system the light mountings act as conductors, and should therefore be mounted on a metal part of the frame **4**. Some plastic mudguards have a metal strip running through them for this purpose. If the back light is mounted on a mudguard made of plastic only, an extra wire must be added as a conductor.

Sometimes the dynamo connection can be made via a metal strip in the mudguard. Two wire connections are needed for this: from the dynamo to a bush at the front of the mudguard, and from another bush at the back of the mudguard to the back light itself. Both connections will need checking if the lights fail.

Faults in the system

If one or both lights fail owning to a fault in the dynamo system, then a systematic procedure is required to diagnose and correct the fault. The diagram overleaf is a good example of such a procedure.

It is impossible to give proper instructions for every case, as there are so many totally different systems, and the accessibility of bulbs and contacts varies enormously.

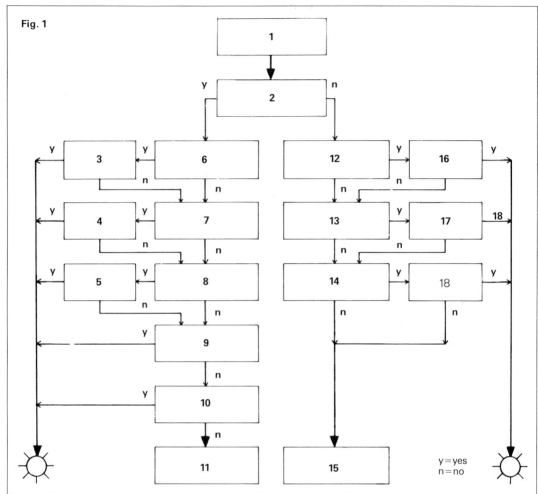

Fig. 1

Number	What is wrong/What to do
1	The front or back light won't work
2	Is the other light working?
3	Clean and tighten the contact − OK now?
4	Clean and tighten the mounting − OK now?
5	Fix the bulb more firmly − OK now?
6	Is the contact loose or dirty?
7	Is the mounting loose or dirty?
8	Is the bulb loose?
9	Replace the bulb - OK now?
10	Replace the wire - OK now?
11	Replace the light
12	Is the dynamo contact faulty?
13	Is the dynamo mounting faulty?
14	Is the wiring short-circuiting?
15	Replace the dynamo
16	Clean and tighten the contact − OK now?
17	Clean and tighten the mounting − OK now?
18	Reinsulate or replace the wiring − OK now?

Fig. 2

Fig. 3

Fig. 4

Figures ❷ and ❸, for example, show how to replace a bulb in just one kind of back light.

You should always carry spare lightbulbs with you. They are best wrapped in paper and kept inside the tyre-repair kit. The usual ratings are 6V and 2.4W (0.4A) for a front lightbulb, 6V and 0.6W (0.1A) for a back lightbulb. Halogen bulbs give out more light for the same capacity, and keep their brightness for a much longer time. But they are mounted differently, and can only be used with a special light fitting.

The commonest fault is when a contact comes loose and breaks the circuit. Modern spring-loaded contacts work much better if the wire is soldered at the end (see page 15). The insulation must be cut back about 1cm from the end so that the wire is properly exposed. A contact ring should also if possible be soldered to the end of the wire.

If the bulb and contacts are OK and the light still won't work, this means the wire is probably broken inside the insulation and the whole wire needs to be replaced. Make sure the new wire is long enough to provide at least 10cm of spare wire with the handlebars fully locked; this allows for sHortening if the contacts have to be repaired. When replacing a wire that runs along inside the frame, solder the new wire to the old one and pull the new wire into position as you pull the old wire out.

The commonest dynamo fault is when the roller slips on the tyre. This happens especially in wet weather. There are tyres that are specially corrugated along the side to help the roller turn more effectively; these should be mounted so that the corrugation comes in contact with the roller. It may also help to bring the dynamo closer to the tyre so as to improve the contact. There are also special rubber caps that you can place over the roller to prevent it from slipping.

Back-wheel dynamo

There is one type of dynamo that runs on the back wheel instead of the front wheel. It is mounted immediately behind the bottom bracket below the chainstays ❹, and the roller runs along the tread of the tyre. The system works more efficiently and creates less resistance to the rider. But it is also more liable to go wrong, because the roller slips very easily.

One way of preventing this is to wrap a piece of old tyre inner tube around the roller (the roller mountings must be temporarily unscrewed on one side in order to do this).

Another way is to run a strong rubber band between the roller mountings and rear drop-outs so as to improve the contact between the roller and the tyre.

Reflectors

The secondary lighting system consits of reflectors that shine back the light from vehicles coming up behind. They become less effective if moisture gets inside them, so a cracked or broken reflector must always be replaced ☐.

Accessories

It is impossible to give full maintenance instructions for every possible bike accessory. One can do no more than point out some of the main things to watch out for.

The following items are dealt with specifically: mudguards, luggage rack, chainguard, prop stand, speedometer, bell and tyre pump. But before that there are some general points that can be made.

Firstly, not all bike accessories are as useful in practice as the manufacturers say they are. Don't hesitate to remove anything that is impracticable to use; if possible try to avoid mounting such items in the first place.

Also take careful note of all instructions (if any) provided by the manufacturers. If any accessories were already mounted when you bought the bike, you should ask the dealer for instructions. This applies especially to items with moving parts such as a speedometer, but also to more specialised items such as a chain case.

All accessories with moving parts must be cleaned, greased and adjusted as regularly as

Fig. 1

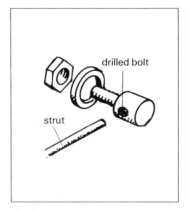

drilled bolt

strut

Fig. 2

Fig. 3

any other part of the bike. Anything that is not fixed in at least two places will come loose with time. So fix everything in two places, even when this is not specified by the manufacturer. Tighten or replace all loose nuts and bolts (acorn nuts may help to keep them tight).

Parts that are clamped to tubes always hold better if a patch is stuck over the appropriate place before the clamp is mounted. Clean the tube, apply rubber solution and let it dry a little before sticking on the patch in the same way as you would a tyre patch. If you need a large

patch, you can make one out of a piece of inner tube; but you should first cover it with rubber solution and let that dry for about three minutes.

Mudguards

You will occasionally need to tighten the bolts that secure the mudguard struts to the drop-outs. The same applies to the bolts holding the struts to the mudguard.

If a mudguard needs straightening or is rubbing against the wheel, then this can be corrected as follows: loosen the bolts at the drop-outs,

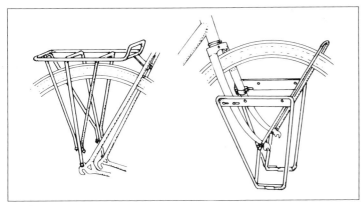

Fig. 4

Fig. 5

sturdier. A decent luggage rack should consist of a stable framework of struts and bars, either of thick metal tubing or of strong steel wire (6mm plus) or aluminium wire (8mm plus) welded to form a triangular structure **4**. The securing bolts should be regularly checked, tightened and where necessary replaced.

The struts of the rear luggage rack are bolted directly to the drop-outs, and are placed under rather than over the mudguard struts if both are attached to the same lugs. Washers should be inserted as usual under both the nut and the bolt head. The rack should be firmly fixed to the seat stays or seat-stay bridge, if necessary with a clamp (after sticking patches around the stays).

A front luggage rack is attached in two places: to the brake mountings at the top **5**, and below either bolted to the drop-outs or clamped to the front forks.

Chainguard

Most bikes have a chainguard on one side only. This stops any oil from getting on your clothing, but doesn't protect the chain from water or dirt. The 'conventional' or 'policeman's' bike, on the other hand, has a completely encased chainguard that offers much better protection. This is known as a chain case.

Although some new chainguards are supplied with suitable fitting instructions, there are always problems

adjust the position of the struts until the mudguards are straight, and finally tighten the bolts again **3**.

Drilled bolts are the type normally used. Figure **2** shows the order in which the relevant components are mounted. If simple bolts are used, then washers should be inserted both under the nut and between the strut and the bolt head.

The mudguard struts on a policeman's bike are held around the wheel axle and under the wheel-nut washer. Their position cannot be adjusted, and bending them is

the only way to straighten the mudguards.

Luggage rack

Unfortunately the minimum requirements or lugguage racks are so low that many of them will bend or even collapse under the weight of luggage. Two notable exceptions are the racks supplied with policeman's bikes and aluminium bikes from Kettler.

If a rack needs to carry anything heavier than a picnic basket or a satchel, then the standard issue should be replaced by something much when a chainguard is added to a bike that has never had one previously. It is never quite compatible with the transmission, and grindings and clatterings are the inevitable result. So if possible a new chainguard should only be fitted as a replacement for an old, damaged one.

The mountings are the main problem area, and should be regularly checked and tightened; clamp and slide fittings should be similarly adjusted and straightened. If the chainguard gets in the way of the chain, chainwheel or wheel, then the mountings must be checked and adjusted or even bent back if necessary

The chain case on a policeman's bike must first be opened up for this purpose. It is not usually very difficult to work out how this is done. Standard plastic chain cases of the De Woerd type can be easily taken apart. There are two plastic pegs shaped like screws at the back and the front. These should be turned through 90° and taken out. All the other parts are held together by clamps, which can be removed one by one.

The chain case only needs to be partly opened up to get at the chain. If all that needs doing is to lubricate the chain or check the chain tension, then you simply have to remove one of the slide fittings in the middle section; it can just be flexed and pulled out.

Prop stand

The one-legged prop stand is the commonest form, but the

Fig. 1

Fig. 2

two-legged models provide greater stability and better balance. Both types are fixed between the chainstays, either with a simple hexagonal bolt and locking plate, or with an 8mm allen bolt screwed into a flat mounting plate.

A one-legged prop stand often works loose; it then gets in the way of the cranks or the wheel, and doesn't prop the

bike up properly. This problem can be easily avoided by regularly tightening the mounting bolt. Thus the otherwise rarely used 8mm allen key becomes a worthwhile investment **1**. If the bike still won't stand correctly, the prop stand may have to be shortened with a hacksaw.

Some two-legged models become splayed under the

Fig. 3

Fig. 4: Bending the bell striker

Tyre speedometers must be regularly cleaned. On modern plastic models the rollers and bearings should be cleaned with water. On old-fashioned metal models the bearings and turning shaft must be lubricated with light oil. The wheel must be straight and the tyre must exert exactly the right pressure on the roller. Sometimes the roller position has to be adjusted to correct this. To increase the pressure, loosen the wheel slightly, bend the roller in towards the tyre, and tighten up the wheel again.

Hub speedometers **2** must be lubricated once a month. The bike must be turned upside-down for this purpose, placing the handlebars carefully so that nothing is bent or damaged. Afterwards the stopper should be replaced in the lubricating nipple **3**. If the speedometer malfunctions, the turning shaft must be removed, lubricated and reinstalled.

The bell

The bell must be firmly attached and easy to reach from the normal hand position on the bars. You should occasionally unscrew the shell and lightly oil the mechanism underneath. This does not, however, apply to racing bikes, which have a single striker that is activated directly.

If the bell doesn't ring properly, see if the shell is touching a brake cable or other mounting. If not, try bending the striker a little inwards or outwards **4**.

weight of the bike and its rider. The simplest solution is to pull the legs together with a piece of metal chain.

The flat mounting plate can easily become bent. This problem can be solved by making a piece of 3–4mm thick steel of the same size with a 10mm hole in it, and bolting it between the prop stand and the mounting plate. Don't forget to add the washer as well.

Speedometer

There are three kinds of speedometer: electronic speedometers, those with a roller wheel that runs along the side of the tyre, and those that run from a sprocket attached to the front hub. Electronic speedometers should be mounted and used according to the manufacturer's instructions.

Tyre pump

Tyre pumps are fitted with different valve connections for use with different kinds of tyre valve (see page 52). The so-called 'racing pump' is intended for Presta valves, but can also be used with the traditional Woods valves; however, a pump for a Woods valve cannot be used with Presta valves. The car-type valves that are used on BMX and mountain bikes can only be inflated with the correct pump (or with an air pump at a filling station).

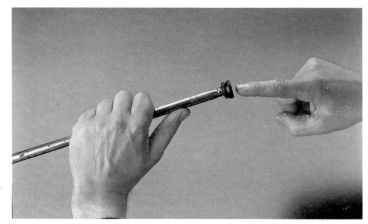

Fig. 1

Some pumps can in some cases be supported between the tubes of the frame. Otherwise a special tyre-pump bracket must be mounted on the frame **3**.

There are two main faults that can affect tyre pumps: lack of compression and escaping air. The first of these is apparent when the pumping action creates no tangible resistance. This is normally due to a faulty leather at the end of the piston **1**. You should open up the pump and rub vegetable fat into the leather (or if necessary replace it), and finally screw everything back again.

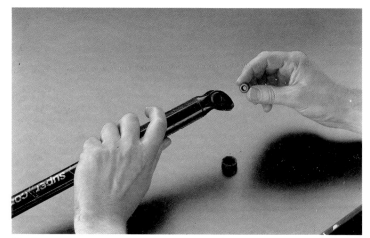

Fig. 2

If air is escaping, this sometimes indicates a leak in the outer casing. But it is most often due to a loose ring in the valve connection. You should first try tightening the cap, which compresses the ring. If that doesn't work, then the ring must be replaced **2**; screw the cap back on afterwards.

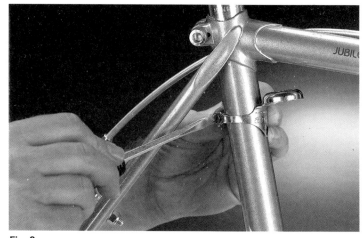

Fig. 3

Appendix

Troubleshooter's guide

Symptom	Possible causes	Probable cure	See pages
Riding is impeded (when pedalling or freewheeling)	1. Tyre pressure too low 2. Wheel bearings wrongly adjusted 3. Wheel is touching frame	Inflate tyre Adjust or overhaul hub Straighten or adjust wheel	52/104 58 56/59
Riding is impeded (only when pedalling)	1. Chain is worn, wrongly adjusted or needs lubricating 2. Bottom bracket wrongly adjusted or needs greasing 3. Pedal wrongly adjusted or needs greasing 4. Chain or chainwheel touching frame	Overhaul chain Adjust or overhaul bottom bracket Adjust or overhaul pedal Tighten chain or straighten chainwheel	48 37–42 46 47
Steering is pulling in one direction	1. Wheels out of track 2. Headset wrongly adjusted 3. Front forks are bent 4. Frame is bent	Straighten wheels Overhaul headset Straighten forks Straighten frame	56/59 24 29 22
Unpleasant vibrations	1. Rim is bent 2. Tyre badly worn down 3. Headset is loose 4. Hub bearings are loose	Straighten wheel Replace tyre Adjust headset Adjust hub bearings	59 55 23 58
Unpleasant noises when pedalling	1. Chainwheel, crank or pedal is loose 2. Chain is worn or needs lubricating 3. Bottom bracket or pedal bearings are loose	Tighten or replace Overhaul or replace Adjust or overhaul	42–47 48 37/46
Chain slips or jumps	1. New chain fitted on old sprocket 2. Chain (with split link) is worn or very loose 3. Chainlink is stiff or damaged	Replace sprocket Adjust or replace chain Loosen or replace chainlink	82/92 47 48

Symptom	Possible causes	Probable cure	See pages
Chain slips off sprocket or chainwheel	1. Changer is wrongly adjusted	Adjust changer	83
	2. Chainwheel is loose	Tighten chainwheel	47
	3. Chain is worn or too long	Replace or shorten chain	49
	4. Chainline is out	Correct chainline	50
Pedalling irregular	1. Pedal axle is bent	Replace pedal	45
	2. Crank is bent	Straighten or replace crank	42 – 44
	3. Bottom bracket is loose	Adjust bottom bracket	37/40
	4. Pedal bearings are loose	Adjust pedal bearings	46
Individual derailleur gears won't engage	1. Changer is badly adjusted	Adjust changer	83
	2. Changer is dirty or damaged	Clean and lubricate or replace changer	83
	3. Cable is wrongly adjusted or defective	Adjust or replace cable	86
	4. Gear lever is loose or defective	Tighten or replace lever	87
	5. Cable guides or mountings are loose	Tighten cable guides or mountings	86
Individual hub gears won't engage	1. Adjusting barrel set badly	Correct adjustment	79
	2. Cable is trapped or cable guides are loose	Replace cable or tighten cable guides	81
	3. Gear lever is defective	Replace lever	81
	4. Gear hub is defective or wrongly adjusted	Lubricate hub, adjust bearings, overhaul hub	81
Rim brakes delayed or not working	1. Cable tension badly adjusted	Adjust cable	67
	2. Quick-release inadvertently open	Close quick-release	67
	3. Rim is dirty	Clean rim	67
	4. Rubber blocks running on wet steel rims	Use aluminium rims or special blocks	71
	5. Inner or outer cable is trapped	Free trapped cable and lubricate or replace it	70
	6. Brake mechanism loose or defective	Tighten and lubricate or overhaul brakes	68/72
	7. Blocks badly adjusted	Adjust blocks	67/71
	8. Levers are loose or defective	Adjust or replace levers	74

Symptom	Possible causes	Probable cure	See pages
Rim brakes are juddering	1. Rim is dirty or damaged 2. Brake mechanism loose 3. Blocks loose or wrongly adjusted 4. Headset loose	Clean or replace rim Tighten mounting or pivot bolt Tighten and adjust blocks Adjust headset	67/62 · 72 71 23
Rim brakes are noisy	See points 1, 2 and 3 above		
Back-pedal brake delayed or not working	1. Anchor plate is loose 2. Hub needs lubricating 3. Hub bearings wrongly adjusted 4. Chain is defective 5. Hub is defective	Tighten anchor plate Lubricate hub Adjust hub bearings Remount or replace chain Overhaul or replace hub	74 75 75 48/49 58/62
Back-pedal brake is jerky	1. Anchor plate not properly fixed to clamp or down tube 2. Hub needs lubricating 3. Hub bearings wrongly adjusted 4. Hub is defective	Fasten anchor plate with appropriate clamp Lubricate hub Adjust hub bearings Overhaul or replace hub	74 75 75 58/62
Drum brakes delayed or not working	1. Lever and cable problems: see 'Rim brakes' points 1, 5 and 8 opposite 2. Anchor plate is loose 3. Water or oil in brake drum 4. Brake linings worn	Tighten anchor plate Overhaul brakes and maybe replace brake linings Replace brake linings	76 76
Dynamo system faulty	1. Dynamo slipping (especially in wet weather) 2. Faulty bulb 3. Faulty wire or contact 4. Faulty mountings 5. Insulation is defective (short-circuiting)	Adjust roller position, bend mounting inwards Replace bulb Check wires and contacts, maybe replace wire Establish metal contact Free trapped wires and reinsulate	76 96 99 99 97 99

Ballbearing measurements

Location of bearings	Ballbearing size	
	inches	millimetres
Bottom bracket	¼ "	about 6.4mm
Rear hub	¼ "	about 6.4mm
Front hub (except Campagnolo Record and Zeus Weltmeister)	$^3/_{16}$ "	about 4.8mm
Front hub (Campagnolo Record and Zeus Weltmeister)	$^7/_{32}$ "	about 5.6mm
Headset (except Zeus, Campagnolo and Shimano Dura Ace)	$^5/_{32}$ "	about 4.0mm
Headset (Zeus, Campagnolo and Shimano Dura Ace)	$^3/_{16}$ "	about 4.8mm
Pedals	$^5/_{32}$ "	about 4.0mm
Freewheel	$^1/_8$ "	about 3.2mm

Observations:
1. Nowadays sealed bearings are occasionally used. The ballbearings cannot be changed in these. If anything goes wrong the whole bearing must be replaced, and this is a job for the expert.
2. The millimetre conversion is not quite exact, an inch being equivalent to 25.4mm. All bicycle measurements are in inches.

measure-ment x	ballbearing size
25mm	$^1/_8$ "
36mm	$^5/_{32}$ "
38mm	$^3/_{16}$ "
44mm	$^7/_{32}$ "
51mm	¼ "

8 ballbearings

measurement x

Thread measurements

Location of bearings	English	French	Italian	Swiss
Bottom bracket fixed cup*	1.370 x 24TPI (L)***	35 x 1 (R)	36 x 24TPI (R)	35 x 1 (L)
Bottom bracket adjusting cup*	1.370 x 24TPI (R)	35 x 1 (R)	36 x 24TPI (R)	35 x 1 (R)
Left pedal	$^9/_{16}$" x 20TPI (L)	14 x 1.25 (L)	English	
Right pedal	$^9/_{16}$" x 20TPI (R)	14 x 1.25 (R)	English	
Headset*	1" x 24TPI	25 x 1	25.4 x 24TPI	
Freewheel/rear hub	1.370 x 24TPI	34.7 x 1	35 x 24TPI	
Drop-outs/derailleur mountings**	(French)	10 x 1	10 x 26TPI	

Observations:
* Basic models from the TI-Raleigh group (Raleigh, Rudge, BSA, Humber, Phillips) have their own specific standards for the headset)1" x 26TPI and bottom bracket)1.375" x 26TPI.
** Some drop-outs have a threadless hole for mounting the changer.
***L = left-hand thread; R = right-hand thread.

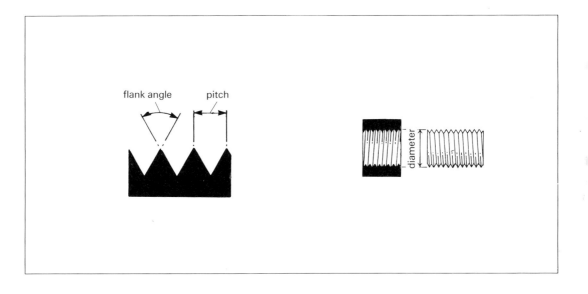

Index